IMAGES
of America

INDIAN RIVER
COUNTY

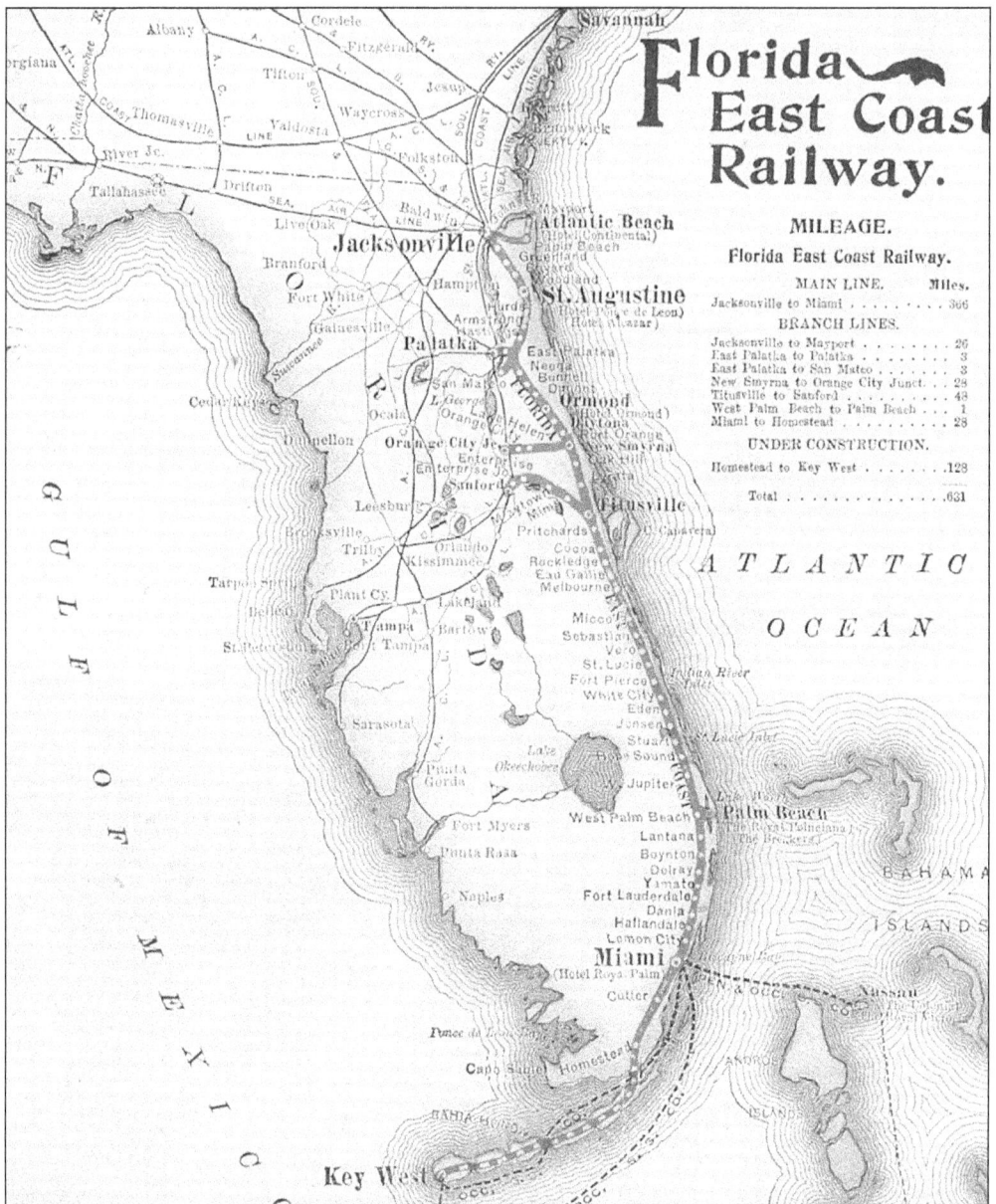

FLORIDA EAST COAST RAILWAY, 1908. In 1893–1894, Florida East Coast Railway completed laying track through the Indian River County area. Very quickly, people and commercial enterprises adopted this fast, easy, less-expensive method of travel for Florida. It fostered major changes, as it boosted population growth. Railroad was the death-knell of the steamboat. Local workers prospered during these years, employed in the clearing of land and laying of tracks. (MAL.)

ON THE COVER: LUMBER INDUSTRY, PIONEERING VERO. Early Vero was a beehive of activity. Land was cleared for farms and groves, and the timber was milled for homes as the new settlers poured into Vero. In 1916, Vero had two sawmills, Indian River Saw Mill Company and Redstone Lumber and Supply, owned and operated by the Charles Gilbert Redstone family. The Redstones had horses and 15 yokes of oxen hauling lumber. (TY.)

IMAGES
of America

INDIAN RIVER
COUNTY

Ellen E. Stanley

ARCADIA
PUBLISHING

Copyright © 2010 by Ellen E. Stanley
ISBN 978-1-5316-5776-5

Published by Arcadia Publishing
Charleston, South Carolina

Library of Congress Control Number: 20100924490

For all general information contact Arcadia Publishing at:
Telephone 843-853-2070
Fax 843-853-0044
E-mail sales@arcadiapublishing.com
For customer service and orders:
Toll-Free 1-888-313-2665

Visit us on the Internet at www.arcadiapublishing.com

CONTENTS

Acknowledgments   6

Introduction   7

1.   Barrier Islands   9

2.   Roseland and the St. Sebastian River Area   21

3.   Sebastian   29

4.   Blue Cypress Lake   39

5.   Fellsmere Farms Company   45

6.   Fellsmere   57

7.   Wabasso   69

8.   Indian River Farms Company   85

9.   Vero Beach   97

10.   Indian River County   115

Bibliography   126

Index   127

ACKNOWLEDGMENTS

I would like to thank the following individuals and institutions for their assistance in the making of this book: special thanks to Pamela J. Cooper, supervisor of the Archive Center and Genealogy Department at the Indian River County Main Library. This book would not have been possible without her valuable assistance. Also thanks to the members of the Indian River Genealogical Society for their help. Most valuable of all were the many donors who provided these images, including Gayle Brown, Dorothy O'Guinn, Bruce Smith, Beverly Tyson, and Tony Young. The complete list is given below.

KEY FOR PHOTOGRAPH SOURCE INFORMATION
Collections in the Archive Center, Indian River County Main Library:
HIL—Arthur Mayfield Hill Collection
IRCHS—Indian River County Historical Society Collection
IRCHS-KOR—Clarence "Korky" Korker Collection of IRC Historical Society
KEY—George Keyes Photograph Donation (Library of Congress)
KOR—Clarence "Korky" Korker Collection
MAC—Mack Collection (Heritage Center)
MAL—Janet W. and James A. Malcolm Collection
NAS—U.S. Naval Air Station Collection
NEL—George Nelson Collection
NIS—Nisle Digital Images Collection
OGU—Nancy O'Guinn Photograph Collection
SEL—Sell Collection (John and Polly Willis)
SIE—Walter A. Siewert Collection
SMI—Estate of Bruce J. Smith Collection
SX—Waldo Sexton Collection
TIP—Tippin Collection (James B. Tippin)
TWI—Twitchell Collection
TY—Tony Young Collection
VAN—Gayle Brown Vandiveer Collection

Other collections:
IRCHS-HH—Hallstrom House, Indian River County Historical Society
LOC—Library of Congress, Prints and Photographs Division, Detroit Publishing Company Collection
PMM—Penobscot Marine Museum, Rudolph Herman Cassens/Eastern Illustrating Company Collection

6

INTRODUCTION

In the late 1800s, Florida was an American frontier. The adventurers flocked to Florida, much in the same way they went West. From the tales that filtered into the north about Florida, it had it all: good pasturage, fertile soil, mild winters, abundant game and fish, free land, heroic soldiers, and Native Americans. The Indian River County area was no exception. It drew a constant stream of those adventurous souls.

The Seminole Wars (1817–1858) and Civil War (1861–1865) had a great influence on the settlement of Florida. The presence of the military over such extended periods of time provided stability and some substantial roads. Forts became towns. Many soldiers became settlers. Removal of most of the Native Americans in 1858 allayed the fears of prospective settlers. The Homestead Act of 1862 granted 160 acres of land.

Wondrous tales and pictures of untamed Florida excited interest. Published accounts such as those of Dr. James A. Henshall in 1878, Andrew Canova in 1885, and Dr. George W. Holmes in 1891 were popular. They described a fertile wilderness, teeming with an astonishing array of plants, wildlife, fish, and insects. Photographers William Henry Jackson, George Nelson, and others provided images. The promoters of the 1890s advertised profits of citrus culture and farming. The Indian River area was touted for its healthy, mild climate and as an escape from northern winters. All of these lures proved to be irresistible, and people flocked to the area.

But travel through the state was formidable. Before the railroad was completed, travel was often long and arduous, a combination of travel by land and water, by means of horse, wagon, on foot, by ship, sailboat, or steamboat. Personal belongings and goods purchased from the north traveled in this same complicated fashion, as did commercial produce sent north.

Florida's generous 1893 land grant law allowed 8,000 acres to be claimed for every mile of railroad built. Henry Flagler's grant eventually was in excess of 2 million acres. The track for the Florida East Coast Railway was laid through the county in 1893–1894.

Slowly, roads were cut through the county. In 1893–1894, Henry Gifford and Sam Hughes created a county road from Fort Pierce to Wabasso. They were paid $22.50 a mile for cutting trees, grubbing stumps, and clearing out undergrowth.

Nature had a part to play in shaping the county. Hurricanes contributed to the many shipwrecks that deposited survivors and wreckage all along the county coastline, prompting the establishment of Houses of Refuge along the Florida East Coast in the late 1800s, including one at Bethel Creek. The freezes of 1894–1895 improved fishing by destroying some undesirable species; truckloads of dead fish were harvested for fertilizer. However, area freezing and flooding proved to be continuing agricultural disasters.

This area did not become Indian River County until 1925. Prior to that time, it was part of a succession of other counties. Likewise, many areas in the county changed names over time, and growth patterns changed as settlers and developers arrived. Each area has its own unique texture.

Indian River Colony was the first development attempted. A group of 40 men and their families led by Maj. William Russell settled along the eastern shoreline with 160-acre land grants obtained through the 1842 Armed Occupation Act. The colony failed when the other settlers fled after John Barker's death at the hands of Native Americans around 1849.

The next settlers to the Sebastian area were most likely Andrew Canova and Ed Marr in 1858. In 1882, Thomas New obtained a post office and named the area Newhaven. It was changed to Sebastian in 1884. Fishing was a mainstay of the economy. Sebastian incorporated in 1924.

The barrier islands were popular with early settlers, due to the ease of water transportation, rich soil for agriculture, and mild winters. Agricultural commerce shifted more to the west of the Indian River after the advent of the railroads, as transportation shifted from water to rail.

In 1816, a grant of 160 acres was received by George Fleming from the Spanish government in the northern part of the county. Ownership of this land passed to succession of different developers. In 1888, in the north, an area was named Waregan and in the south was a lake named Mendota. In 1903, Berry Land Company took over the sale of land in the Roseland area. It never incorporated.

San Sebastian was a community planned at the north end of the county in 1925. Famed artist Lavon West helped plan and design this lavish Spanish-style community that was never built. Just a few homes and the popular San Sebastian Inn were erected.

Development was planned many times, but not completed for the western part of the county. Lake Wilmington (Blue Cypress Lake) was at the western edge of various development projects. Transportation to this section was very difficult, and projects failed before rail service and roads were completed.

Fellsmere received vigorous promotion and development by Fellsmere Farms Company from 1911 through 1917. Drainage canals, roads, railways, city streets, utilities, and social amenities were created. At one point, the population of Fellsmere was the largest in the county; however, many left Fellsmere during the 1915 flooding and never returned.

Broadmoor was a second town planned by Fellsmere Farms Company 5 miles west of Fellsmere. By July 1915, it had a post office, stores, and a school. It was evacuated due to the severe flooding from rain and never recovered.

George Sears settled in Wabasso in the early 1880s. George King erected the first frame house there. It became a center for citrus and agriculture. Elmer E. Smith and family arrived in 1904 and opened a general store. Wabasso incorporated in 1925 to handle some civic matters and then unincorporated itself.

In the late 1800s, J. T. Gray created a plantation he named Woodley, near the present town of Winter Beach. This name persisted until the post office there was renamed Quay in 1902. Later it became Winter Beach. Early settlers to this truck farming area were Stan Jones, Eli Walker, and William E. Wigfield.

Around the turn of the century, George Hall, Judge Jones, E. W. Hall, John C. Jones, and a few others had plantations in the area west of Quay named Klondike Plantations. It never really developed and eventually lost its identity.

Settlers arrived in Gifford beginning in 1883, with land purchased by Mary Harvey. William Brown and several other families homesteaded in 1896. At one time, Gifford was named Brownsville. The name changed to Gifford in honor of pioneer Henry Gifford.

In the mid- to late 1800s, individuals began settling the Vero area, farming and fishing along the Indian River. After the advent of the railroad in 1893–1894, newcomers settled near the tracks. The third wave of settlers came in 1912, promoted by Indian River Farms Company developers. "Vigorous Vero" grew rapidly and incorporated as Vero Beach in 1925.

Originally Oslo was named Crawford Point, the site of a banana plantation owned by Bough and Barnes Company. The Helseths and Hallstroms were early settlers in the Oslo area around the 1890s. They raised pineapples on the high dry sand ridge. For some time, pineapples outpaced citrus as the major crop.

One

BARRIER ISLANDS

PELICAN ISLAND, 1910. The Barrier Islands lie on the easternmost edge of Indian River County along the Atlantic Ocean. Ease of transportation, temperate climate, and fertile land lured the earliest settlers to these islands. Pelican Island is a natural bird rookery that attracted plume hunters around the turn of the century. It became the first national wildlife refuge in 1903, and Paul Kroegel was its first warden. (IRCHS.)

Dawson's Gem Island. Shown are Ralph and Lewis Dawson Jr. in front of their house. Their father, Lewis Dawson, acquired approximately 133 acres of land in 1884 through the Homestead Act of 1862 and land patents. These two photographs are by William Henry Jackson. (LOC.)

Dawson's House, Gem Island. In 1884, Lewis Dawson brought his wife, Kate, and their children Louis Jr., Ralph, and Louise to the island that was covered in custard apples, sugar apples, and sapodillas. Throughout his land he planted citrus groves. A little store was in his house, and he was postmaster of the Narrows post office, which was commissioned in 1884. A friendly and hospitable man, he welcomed all. (LOC.)

WILLIAM JORDAN BARKER AROUND 1935.
William Jordan Barker was a planter on Orchid
Island in the early 1900s. The postmaster
of Orchid Island was Frank Forster around
that same time. In 1935, Barker lived in
Wabasso. Early pioneers of the Barker clan
were Elisha Luther Barker and his wife,
Rose Ann of Johns Island, who had 13
children. In 1931, they had 51 grandchildren
and 33 great-grandchildren. (VAN.)

CORA BARKER. The daughter of William
Jordan Barker and Lula Frances Hazel,
Cora Lee Barker was born on Orchid
Island in 1902. The Barkers held annual
reunions in Wabasso for the numerous
members of the Barker clan who lived
in Vero, Winter Beach, Wabasso, Fort
Pierce, and Orchid Island. (VAN.)

11

MICHAEL RESIDENCE ON THE INDIAN RIVER. The Stephen Michael and William Wigfield families came to Florida together in 1887. After first looking at the West Coast, George King convinced them to try the East Coast where they met Capt. Frank Forster. They each purchased 5 acres from Captain Forster on Orchid Island. Bananas were the first money crop for the Michaels, and later they grew citrus and vegetables. (IRCHS.)

STEPHEN MICHAEL HOUSE. Soon after arriving in 1887, Stephen Michael began building his house on Orchid Island with lumber shipped down from Titusville. It was one of the first two-story houses in the area. His wife, Laura, and seven children arrived in September 1887. In 1902, son Alfred Benjamin Michael bought his parents' house, and his parents moved to Orange County. (IRCHS.)

PICNIC AT THE MICHAELS. The Michaels threw a picnic on the lawn on February 13, 1910, with their neighbors. But life was not all picnics. When Jack Spratt's kitchen roof caught fire in September 1888, he yelled, "Fire!" Steven Michael made it in the fastest time, a quarter mile in three minutes, ahead of Mr. Wier and Edward Michael. They managed to save the house with buckets of water. (VAN.)

WIGFIELD HOUSE. William Wigfield arrived from West Virginia in 1887 with seven daughters. In 1891, he purchased land on Orchid Island from Capt. Frank Forster for $200. He built this house there with lumber from Titusville. In 1892, it was torn down and relocated by oxcart and raft to property at Kings Highway, Old Dixie Highway, and Fifty-eighth Street, now Hawks' Nest Golf Course. (IRCHS.)

ORCHID ISLAND SCHOOL. The first school on Orchid Island was erected in 1892. Heron Sykes built an Orchid School in 1913 with materials supplied by Alfred B. Michael. The school was a one-room wooden structure with wooden walks that connected the school to the outhouses. It had a school bell hanging in the front facing the Indian River. Students arrived on foot or by boat. (IRCHS.)

ORCHID SCHOOL TERM 1917–1918. Pictured on the left is teacher Easter M. Russell. In the background on the right is an outhouse. Students purchased their own books and supplies. They brought lunches from home and ate out under the trees or on the porch. The desks had inkwells, but no ink. Grades one through eight were taught. Exemplary students were allowed to ring the school bell. (VAN.)

REAMS HOUSE, JOHNS ISLAND, AROUND 1903. The Reams family is standing in front of its house. After William Reams and Susan married around 1891 on Gem Island, they moved to Johns Island. There they had six children and raised vegetables. Their produce was sent north by steamboat until the railroad came through. William's brother Calvin came to Johns Island at the same time, and they both built their first homes there. (IRCHS.)

TREASURE COAST. More than just fish have been taken from the Atlantic Ocean here. "Treasure Coast" refers to the numerous sailing ships that foundered off the county's coastline, including the famous 1715 Spanish Plate Fleet. After a storm, it is still possible to pick up bits of wreckage and coins. One story relates that a man used over 1,000 silver pieces of eight as skipping stones years ago. (IRCHS.)

LEWIS STOECKEL HOUSE. Bavarian-born Louis Stoeckel resided in Ohio and Connecticut before he obtained a land grant in 1891 for 170 acres in the area of present-day Riomar where he raised vegetables for a living. His brother Gus joined him there. Both were bachelors. From 1913 to 1919, the 170 acres were sold, as the area had become too crowded for them. Herman Zeuch purchased the residence. (IRCHS.)

RIOMAR BEACH CLUB. In August 1929, the construction contract for a new Riomar Club House was given by manager Alec MacWilliam to William Hensick to be completed by January 1, 1930. The two-story Spanish-style building had a stucco-and-tile exterior and an interior finished with pecky cypress walls and oak floors. The former clubhouse was remodeled as a guesthouse. Elaborate landscaping supplied the finishing touch. (IRCHS.)

JUDGE DIAMOND'S HOUSE ON ATLANTIC BOULEVARD. Col. C. P. Diamond and his wife moved from Perry, Florida, where he was a practicing attorney, to Vero Beach in 1925. That same year, he set up law offices in the Seminole Building, became a charter member of the Optimist Club, and was chosen to be adjutant of Felix Poppel Post of the American Legion. (IRCHS.)

DRIFTWOOD INN AIR TOUR, JUNE 28, 1935. Flamboyant and eccentric Waldo Sexton was a very capable businessman. The Driftwood Inn was one of Waldo Sexton's many business ventures. Other businesses he was involved with included the Ocean Grill, the Patio, and the Turf Club restaurants. He was also instrumental in the formation of McKee Jungle Gardens, Vero Beach Dairy, and Oslo Hammock Corporation, among many others. (IRCHS.)

VERO BEACH YACHT BASIN, 1930s. In 1923, word that the Florida East Coast Canal Transportation Company intended to improve the East Coast waterway for commercial shipping prompted years of discussion over creation of a municipal commercial dock. One suggestion was to place it at the end of Osceola Boulevard, another, to put it near the bridge. Another was to put it on the east side of the Indian River. (IRCHS.)

CANOE ON THE INDIAN RIVER, AROUND 1923. This canoe was completely sealed in, impervious to water, the weather, and the hoards of mosquitoes that infested the region at that time. Note the lanterns as well. Mosquito pest control came into consideration in the 1920s in Florida due to concern with the diseases they carried. Early control attempts were often ineffective, however, until the use of DDT after World War II. (IRCHS.)

BOATING ON THE INDIAN RIVER. This picture is one of a group of images found in an abandoned Vero Beach house in 1986 by Joel Dobbs. After research, it was determined that the house had been owned by Arthur M. Hill, a pioneer and entrepreneur of Indian River County. The Hills made frequent excursions by boat to Pelican Island. This picture may have been taken in the 1920s. (HIL.)

FISHING SHACK ON THE INDIAN RIVER. Fishing was a sure method of fast, easy cash for early pioneers. An abundance of fish, oysters, and turtles was caught and shipped north. The bad freezes of 1894–1895 improved the fishing, as it killed off the worthless catfish and toadfish, leaving mullet and trout alive. Dead fish were hauled from the shore by the wagonload and used for fertilizer. (VAN.)

BETHEL CREEK HOUSE OF REFUGE. Due to the large number of shipwrecks on the Florida coast, the U.S. government authorized the construction of five "Houses of Refuge" on Florida's east coast as temporary shelter for shipwrecked individuals. This one at Bethel Creek Inlet was completed in 1876 by Albert Blaisdell. John Houston was appointed as its first keeper that same year. (VAN.)

BETHEL CREEK HOUSE OF REFUGE AFTER MODIFICATIONS. Charles Stoeckel was the keeper in 1885. He was a brother of Lewis Stoeckel who lived on the barrier island opposite Vero. Capt. Walter Kitching was the keeper when the fire occurred in 1917, and the building was destroyed. At that time, it was the Bethel Creek Coast Guard Station, the status having been changed by law two years earlier. (VAN.)

Two

Roseland and the
St. Sebastian
River Area

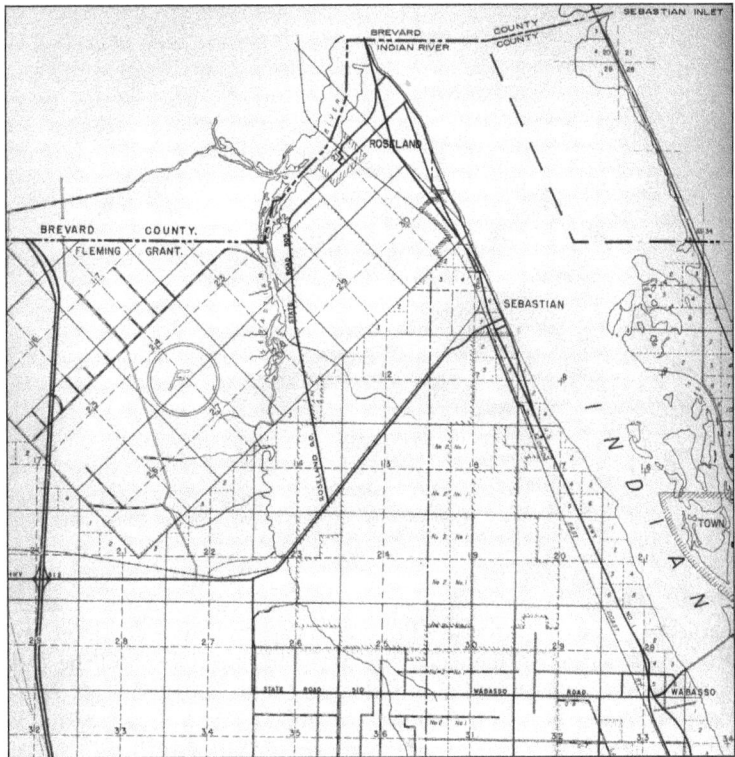

Map of Fleming Grant, Roseland. Roseland is situated in the northeastern part of the Indian River County area on the banks of the St. Sebastian River, which meanders almost wholly within the Fleming Grant. Dempsey Cain, Capt. D. G. Gibson, August Park, and John Baird were early settlers in the Roseland area around 1884. In 1903, Berry Land Company sparked development of Roseland. (CAR.)

ERCILDOUNE PLANTATION. The Ercildoune Plantation, owned by Lawrence Moore, consisted of the Ercildoune Hotel and the Frost Proof Grove consisting of 500 bearing citrus trees that were planted some years before the hotel's opening. No doubt because of its favorable location, the grove was not damaged by the freezes of 1894 and 1895 and remained in good condition into the 1920s. (SIE.)

ERCILDOUNE HOTEL, MOORE'S POINT. Chicagoan Lawrence Moore erected his Ercildoune Hotel on a bluff at the confluence of the St. Sebastian River and the Indian River in 1889. It was constructed of cypress and pine and had a central lobby with a coquina fireplace. Plumbing was exterior. Pres. Grover Cleveland was a popular guest. It closed around World War I and thereafter was taken over by squatters and moonshiners. (SIE.)

SAN SEBASTIAN SIGN. San Sebastian Development Corporation was in business from 1925 to 1936, when it dissolved. It designed San Sebastian to be an old Spanish-styled city on 18,000 acres of land formerly occupied by the Ercildoune Hotel at the north end of the county. It owned the San Sebastian Inn, a popular dining spot, and the development also had a baseball team, golf course, and several residents. (IRCHS.)

SAN SEBASTIAN LABEL. Artist Lavon F. West was the designer, publicity manager, and photographer for San Sebastian. West formulated the style and design of the city through his sketches of Spanish art and architecture. The former Ercildoune Hotel became the barracks for the 180-man work crew. The city that never materialized was planned for the north side of San Sebastian Bay with industrial, commercial, and residential sections. (IRCHS.)

A FAMILY OUTING, SEBASTIAN INLET, JANUARY 1919. Then as now, families were enjoying trips to Sebastian Inlet. This photograph was taken eight months prior to the actual creation of the Sebastian Inlet District, which was formed September 12, 1919, and celebrated with a big party. The estimated cost of creating the inlet was $92,008. By 1929, dredges and barges had been obtained and dynamiting began to open the passage. (IRCHS.)

SEBASTIAN INLET, 1930s STORM. By 1924, a 100-foot-wide channel was completed from the Indian River at its confluence with the St. Sebastian River through the barrier island to the ocean, creating a commercial passageway for both rivers. Although sand fill from periodic storms caused further dredging, it remained open until 1942, when all dredging was halted. A 9-foot-high sand dune formed across the inlet in the following years. (IRCHS.)

WOODEN FERRY. In 1904, when Col. D. S. Martin of Lexington, Kentucky, took his first trip to Florida's east coast by auto, he needed to cross the St. Sebastian River by ferry. While his car was being drawn onto the ferry by a yoke of oxen, one of the oxen took exception to the car and kicked a hole in its radiator with its hind foot. (IRCHS.)

ST. SEBASTIAN RIVER BRIDGE, LOOKING SOUTH. Ferries crossed the St. Sebastian River until this wooden bridge was constructed in 1909 by convicts from the Roseland Convict Camp. This camp supplied labor primarily to local turpentine companies. Leased convict labor was abolished in 1923. In 1924, this bridge was the site of the famous Ashley Gang shoot-out that killed the notorious robbers in an ambush set by the sheriff. (IRCHS.)

ST. SEBASTIAN RIVER, WEST FORK. The St. Sebastian River has two main branches, the south fork and the west fork in the north end of the county. When ornithologist Frank Chapman sailed the St. Sebastian River in 1889, he found a semitropical paradise of morning glories, moonflower blossoms, pines, and tall grass in prairies and flooded meadows with flocks of sand hill cranes, herons, and Carolina parakeets. (SIE.)

STEAMBOAT CLEO, C. 1890. This 50-foot steamboat was the first one built in Brevard County, approximately three years before this photograph was taken. It is seen here on the St. Sebastian River, chartered by photographer William Henry Jackson who captured the early history of the area in his images. He was put ashore by the skiff in the foreground to capture this scene. (KEY.)

ST. SEBASTIAN RIVER. This river lies almost wholly within the Fleming Grant in the northern part of the county. Early travelers found abundant mullet in the shallows and black bass. Quail were plentiful in the palmetto scrub, and the hammocks had many squirrels, raccoons, turkeys, deer, and opossums from the account of Dr. James A. Henshall who sailed down the river in 1879. (IRCHS.)

GRAVES BROTHERS ORANGE GROVES. J. Edwin and Walter F. Graves purchased large tracts of land in Wabasso and the surrounding county in the name of Sebastian Land Company (Selco). In the 1920s and 1930s, Graves Brothers planted 100 acres of citrus in the county. Their first groves were in two long strips on either side of the south fork of the St. Sebastian River. (VAN.)

ST. SEBASTIAN RIVER BRIDGE, SEEN FROM INDIAN RIVER. This panoramic view is looking west from the Indian River to the mainland. Shown is the St. Sebastian River Bridge crossing the St. Sebastian River at its juncture with the Indian River. The wooden bridge over the St. Sebastian River was replaced in 1926 with a concrete span. (IRCHS.)

Three

SEBASTIAN

BARKER'S BLUFF, SEBASTIAN. Situated south of Roseland, Sebastian began as one of the oldest trading posts and fishing villages on the East Coast. A large, ancient Native American mound existed in south Sebastian on the Indian River and was a local landmark for many years. (LOC.)

BARKER'S BLUFF. Photographer William Henry Jackson took this picture of Barker's Bluff (right of center, background) from the steamboat *Cleo*, which he chartered around 1890. The house on the top was believed to be the home of August Park. This white-faced bluff was an immense Ais Indian shell mound. It no longer exists, as it was sold to surface roads between Stuart and Micco in 1908. (LOC.)

PAUL KROEGEL. Attracted by the beauty and wildlife of the area, Gottlob Kroegel and his son Paul settled on 143 acres that included Barker's Bluff, acquired through a land patent in 1889 in south Sebastian. They had a citrus grove and bees and raised vegetables. Their first house was a thatched hut. Paul built his own house in 1899 and married Ila Lawson in 1900. (IRCHS.)

30

GEORGE NELSON HOME, SEBASTIAN. In 1901, George Nelson was employed by the Harvard Museum of Comparative Zoology as a preparator. He was a botanist, taxidermist, zoologist, and photographer. He purchased land from the Kroegel family in 1910 and built a home that he used during his winter trips to Sebastian, where he spent much of his time collecting and photographing specimens. In 1946, he moved to Sebastian. (NEL.)

LET'S GO, C. 1920S. This vehicle is fully loaded and ready to go, as the little sign in the back proclaims. Photographer George Nelson owned a fishing boat in Sebastian named *Let's Go.* George Nelson had a Model T automobile that he used for his trips to Florida, photographing and visiting his friends Paul and Rodney Krogel. They learned photography from him. (IRCHS.)

DIXIE HIGHWAY ENTERING SEBASTIAN, C. 1914. Pictured are the buildings south of Main Street on U.S. Highway 1 looking north. In the foreground is the original Sebastian Town Hall building, erected in 1913. Just north of it is the Bamma Vickers Lawson house and the Stephen Vickers house. They still exist. This section is on the National Register of Historic Places. (PMM.)

SEBASTIAN UNITED METHODIST CHURCH, C. 1914. The members of the United Methodist Church first met in homes of the church members in 1886. In 1889, land was donated by Mr. Howard for a church building at 1029 Main Street. The church was constructed with money raised by members, and its first service was held in 1893. It was enlarged and remodeled in 1901 and completely rebuilt in 1964. (PMM.)

VIEW FROM THE SCHOOL TOWER, SEBASTIAN, C. 1914. This was the view of downtown Sebastian from the tower of the two-story wooden school built in 1904 just west of the Florida East Coast Railway station on Louisiana Avenue. Main Street is on the left running down to the Indian River, and the buildings along U.S. Highway 1 in downtown Sebastian are visible through the trees in the background. (PMM.)

POST OFFICE, MAIN STREET. Shown are Vicker's store (left) and the post office. The first post office in Sebastian was established in 1882 by Thomas New, who called the area Newhaven. In 1884, it was registered by postmaster Sylvanus Kitching as Sebastian. That post office burned to the ground in 1933. The fire also burned the Frederick Park home and two of Dr. David Rose's cottages on Louisiana Avenue. (IRCHS.)

SEBASTIAN TRAIN DEPOT. On May 2, 1912, the *Fellsmere Farmer* announced that due to increased passenger traffic to Sebastian and Fellsmere, Sebastian was made a flag station for the Florida East Coast train operating daily between Jacksonville and Key West. This train had an all-steel mail car, a baggage car, a combination car and coach, and regular Pullman cars. The passenger cars had electric fans and green plush seats. (SMI.)

SEBASTIAN WOMAN'S CLUB. The Sebastian Woman's Club was organized in 1914. The first president was Sarah Wentworth Rose, wife of Dr. Rose. Mrs. Paul Kroegel was recording secretary, and Mrs. George Braddock was first vice president. Their first meetings were in the town hall. In May 1928, the Woman's Club building at 952 U.S. Highway 1 was erected by Paris Lawson and Abraham Foster. (IRCHS.)

SEBASTIAN HOTEL. This wood-frame hotel was built in June 1912 on U.S. Highway 1 north of Main Street next to the post office. Between 1913 and 1927, it was owned successively by Mr. and Mrs. A. C. Arnold, Abraham Stovitz, Jack Salmelia, S. A. Braswell, and Minnie C. Bridges. It was named Hotel Bridges when it burned to the ground January 27, 1927. (IRCHS.)

SEBASTIAN INN. "A charming air of informality pervaded the dining room," according to the *Vero Beach Press* when this inn opened February 18, 1926, located on the shore of the Indian River in Sebastian. Melbourne's foremost orchestra, the Florida Crackers, played symphonic dance music. Although popular for many years, it was torn down in 1968 to build the Sportsman Lodge at that location. (NAS.)

HARDEE HOUSE, SEBASTIAN. The Hardee family moved to Sebastian in 1889. Robert G. Hardee married Clarissa Kitching in 1900 and built this house for her that same year. In 1909, he built another, grander house on Main Street. That one burned in 1936. He owned the yacht *St. Sebastian*, where the family sometimes spent the night. He also owned groves, was a tax assessor, and a Sebastian city councilman. (SIE.)

HARDEE SERVICE STATION. Robert George "Cap" Hardee's service station stood at the corner of Main Street and Indian River Drive in Sebastian. The large tree on the left is the Hardee Oak, planted in 1891 by Hardee. The tree still stands. Hardee also owned the Eagle Company Fish Dock. In May 1913, G. J. Hardee shot and killed Roseland postmaster E. M. Stokes in an argument over baseball. (IRCHS.)

WILLIAM BRADDOCK HOUSE. This brick house was built with a cellar in 1919 by the Wise brothers with materials from the Cocoa area. It is part of the Sebastian section on the National Register of Historic Places. William Braddock was a merchant and grower. His wife, Kate Lawson Braddock, was an organizing member of the Sebastian Woman's Club. (PMM.)

DR. DAVID ROSE. Dr. Rose (second man on right) moved to Florida in 1908. For many years, he was the only doctor between Titusville and Fort Pierce. His home was on Louisiana Avenue, in Sebastian, with a citrus grove in back. With his sailboat, Charlie Sembler took Dr. Rose to house calls along the Indian River. Mainland house calls were by horseback, carriage, or, later, by automobile. (SIE.)

INDIAN RIVER AT SEBASTIAN. Early commerce traveled on the Indian River. Walter Kitching and his 60-foot schooner *Merchant* plied the Indian River, carrying every sort of merchandise from nails to clothes to food. Goods were paid for with gold or silver. A blast on a conch shell alerted customers they were approaching. Three or four of these trade boats plied the river, as did a dentist. (SIE.)

FLOODING IN SEBASTIAN. May 30 through June 6, 1923, was a time of heavy rains. May had over 10 inches of rain, and June had a rainfall of 10 inches in seven days. The ground was completely saturated, and flooding occurred. These rains stopped Sebastian's tomato shipments, and 20 train carloads of tomatoes did not make it out of the fields in time. (IRCHS.)

Four

BLUE CYPRESS LAKE

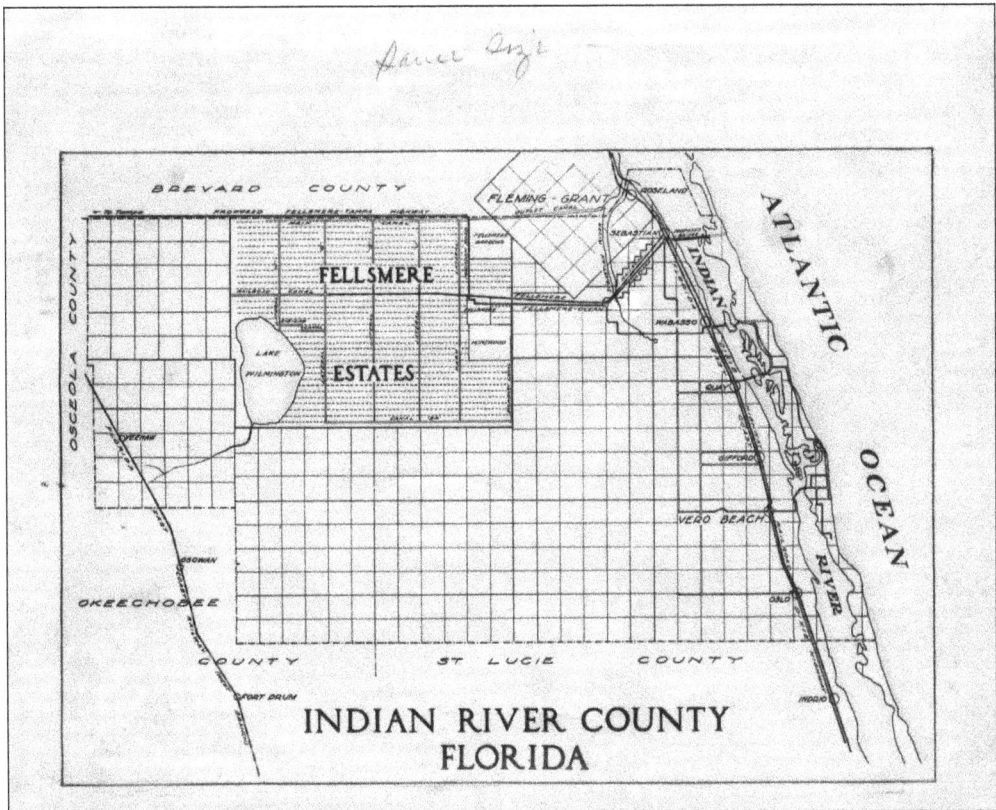

MAP OF INDIAN RIVER COUNTY AFTER 1925. Blue Cypress Lake lies in the western part of Indian River County. The lake and the surrounding marshland were the continued unsuccessful focus of land developers from the 1880s into the early 1900s. The lake received the name Lake Wilmington from developer Anthony Russell in the 1890s. The home of loggers and trappers, the area in 1925 was still isolated, and access was complicated. (SIE.)

CASON'S LANDING ON LAKE WILMINGTON. When Tom Cason moved near Lake Wilmington (Blue Cypress Lake) in the late 1880s, he built a three-room house out of split cypress. During the school year, his wife, Mamie, moved to Osowaw north of Fort Drum so that their seven children could attend school there. Tom made his living by trapping and had a vegetable garden. (SIE.)

ROAD TO CASON'S LANDING, LAKE WILMINGTON. In March 1913, Tom Cason finished his road through the cypress swamp from Lake Wilmington to the prairie west of the lake, a mile west of the Indian Mound. It was a log corduroy road. As well as a trapper, Cason was also much in demand as a guide for hunting parties due to his reliability and extensive knowledge of the area. (SIE.)

LAKE WILMINGTON LOOKING EAST FROM THE INDIAN MOUND. Lake Wilmington was part of land that still had not been surveyed and was sold in 1890 at 50¢ an acre by the Florida Trustees of the Internal Improvement Fund to Willis Palmer, Mathew Marks, and Cecil Butt. They defaulted on the payments, and in 1895, the 115,000-acre tract became the property of Anthony Russell who proposed to develop the area as the Cincinnatus Farm Land Project. (SIE.)

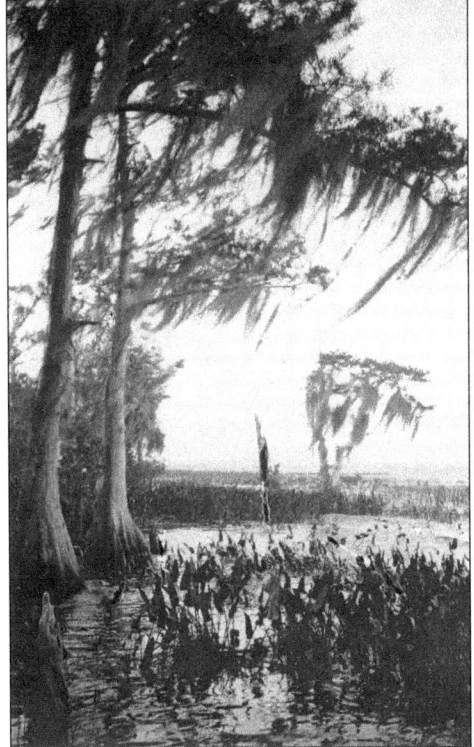

HISTORIC BLUE CYPRESS LAKE. Anthony O. Russell, printer of Bicycle playing cards, obtained the 115,000-acre tract that included the lake he named Lake Wilmington with plans to drain the surrounding marsh, dike the lake, dredge a canal as an outlet for Fort Drum Creek, and lay railroad track to Sebastian. Russell, however, died in 1900, with development only partially completed. (SIE.)

PIONEER HUNTER NEAR LAKE WILMINGTON. On March 11, 1910, E. Nelson Fell made a $63,125 down payment on this marshy, cypress-covered 115,000-acre tract of Florida land that included Lake Wilmington on its western edge. He planned to develop this area by dredging, draining, and diking the land. This became the western part of the Fellsmere Farms Company development with the town of Fellsmere on the eastern edge. (SIE.)

LAND INVESTIGATION TRIP, LAKE WILMINGTON. According to Earl Cason, in the early days before the area began to be developed, it was necessary to go south from Vero to Fort Pierce, across the Alapattah Flats to the west of St. Johns marsh, to the old Military Trail, and take it north to Lake Wilmington, all in order to travel from Vero to Lake Wilmington. (SIE.)

WORK CREW AT LAKE WILMINGTON. The local residents around Lake Wilmington formed a ready work crew for the many jobs created by Fellsmere Farms Company and the Osceola Cypress Company in the 1910s and 1920s. Tom Cason worked building the road west from the lake to the Indian Mound. Raymond Cason was a crane operator digging canals. The men rented out their fishing boats for 50¢ a day. (SIE.)

IN CAMP, WEST SIDE. When John Fries's surveying crew mapped the area in the west part of the county for the Cincinnatus Farm Land Project for owner Anthony Russell in 1895, the whole area was just considered impenetrable swampland, and the lake was unknown. It was surveyed again for the drainage system when Nelson Fell acquired the land for his Fellsmere Farms Company development project in 1910. (SIE.)

LAKE WILMINGTON CAMPSITE. In February 1923, Robert D. Carter and guide W. V. Rogers's journey by boat from Vero to Lake Wilmington was considered an adventure and was reported in the *Vero Press*. They covered 100 miles by boat in five days, traveling on the return trip on the Fellsmere Canal and St. Sebastian River. Snakes, alligators, bears, wildcats, ducks, and whooping cranes were seen along the journey. (SIE.)

LAKE SCENE, BLUE CYPRESS LAKE. It was not until State Road 60 was cut through in 1926 that the west side of the lake was developed. A single-lane dirt road, it was the first direct-access road to that part of the county. In the 1920s, a railroad to the lake was expected but never materialized. Another approach to the lake was by boat via the old Zig Zag Canal. (SIE.)

Five

FELLSMERE FARMS COMPANY

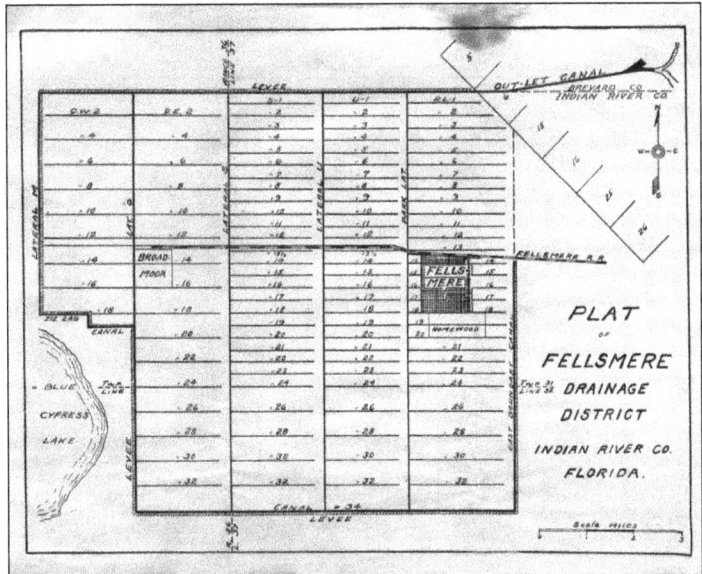

PLAT OF FELLSMERE DRAINAGE DISTRICT. Fellsmere Farms Company planned an ambitious development of the western part of the county, which depended upon the ability to drain the marshland. The design to place a dike around the whole area was considered too expensive. Instead, in 1910, the developers opted to create a series of canals to drain 18,000 acres from Fellsmere to Blue Cypress Lake. (SMI.)

SURVEYOR'S PARTY. The prominent New York engineering firm of J. G. White and Company surveyed and platted the Fellsmere Farms Company land and worked out a drainage plan that consisted of a series of main canals and lateral canals, dredging 7 million cubic feet of earth. Dredging commenced in 1910 with dredges built by the American Steel Dredge Company of Fort Wayne, Indiana. (SIE.)

FELLSMERE FARMS COMPANY ENGINEERS, c. 1915. On the right in the back row is chief engineer Irwin Lloyd with other engineers and visitors. In the front row on the left is Charles Decker and on the farthest right is Ernest H. Every, field manager. Lloyd was the uncle of Germaine and Celeste Dominici. (SIE.)

A SHELL MOUND. Ais Indian shell mounds were prevalent in early county history. The Ais Indian tribes ranged from Cape Canaveral to Jupiter Inlet on the east coast of Florida but mostly had died out by 1760 due to slave raids, disease, and the arrival of Europeans. These middens primarily consisted of oyster shells, coupled with cast-off remains such as broken tools, pottery, and bones. (SIE.)

RICHARD A. CONKLING IN SURREY. The Demonstration Farm was established in 1911 near the railroad on the open prairie where the pine ridge ended, growing a wide variety of vegetables. Conkling was its superintendent. In March 1912, he opened Conkling Nursery with 62,000 orange and grapefruit trees. He also grew ornamental shrubs ready to sell to new Fellsmere residents. This was the first large-scale business organized in Fellsmere. (SIE.)

47

THE GERMAN COLONY. A German colony was established in pioneer Fellsmere. Individuals in Cleveland represented by Edward Kuchenig contracted to purchase tracts of land in Fellsmere from Fellsmere Farms Company. Kuchenig arrived in Fellsmere in August 1913 to begin the process. Here the Germans are beginning to build the Lateral S canal. In the foreground, lumber is being towed by boat for their houses. (SIE.)

GRADING THE ROAD, SEBASTIAN TO FELLSMERE. In August 1912, Richard A. Conkling went before the St. Lucie County commissioners to obtain an appropriation for repairs to the 10-mile road between Sebastian and Fellsmere. Funds were requested to clear the roadway, to fill in low places, and to make it a hard-surfaced boulevard. An appropriation equal to one year's taxes was requested. (SIE.)

48

GRADING THE ROAD FOR FELLSMERE FARMS RAILROAD. The Fellsmere Farms Railroad continued westward from Fellsmere. By February 1912, the railroad bed had been graded westward from Fellsmere beyond the first lateral canal, Lateral U. By April, the railroad was extended west of the second lateral, Lateral S. Railway access enabled the drainage process from Lateral U Canal into the main canal, making 8,000 acres of land available for cultivation. (SIE.)

OUTLET CANAL WORKER'S CAMP. Surveyors began work in 1911, living in tents while they laid out the canal system. By February 1912, the number of workers employed was 175, and they lived under very primitive conditions. Canal workers had these small wooden shacks and tents. Railway workers lived in tents. Eventually a boardinghouse and houses for Ernest Every, Irwin Lloyd, and Richard A. Conkling were built. (SIE.)

FELLSMERE LOGGING. Land was stripped clear with wholesale logging to supply wood for railroad ties and buildings. On January 12, 1913, an uncontrolled prairie fire swept through by the main canal and burned 12,000 feet of lumber destined for the control gates. Five tents and their contents were lost as well. An order was given to East Coast Lumber and Supply Company for replacement lumber. (SIE.)

OXEN HAULING LOGS. These high-wheeled oxen carts were especially useful for hauling logs in soft, moist soil. Several individuals saw the value of setting up sawmills and timbering the land around Fellsmere. Fred Burmeister was interested in building a lumberyard there in 1912. He purchased 193 acres in Fellsmere and began building his home then. In 1916, he was an employee of Fellsmere Farms Company. (SIE.)

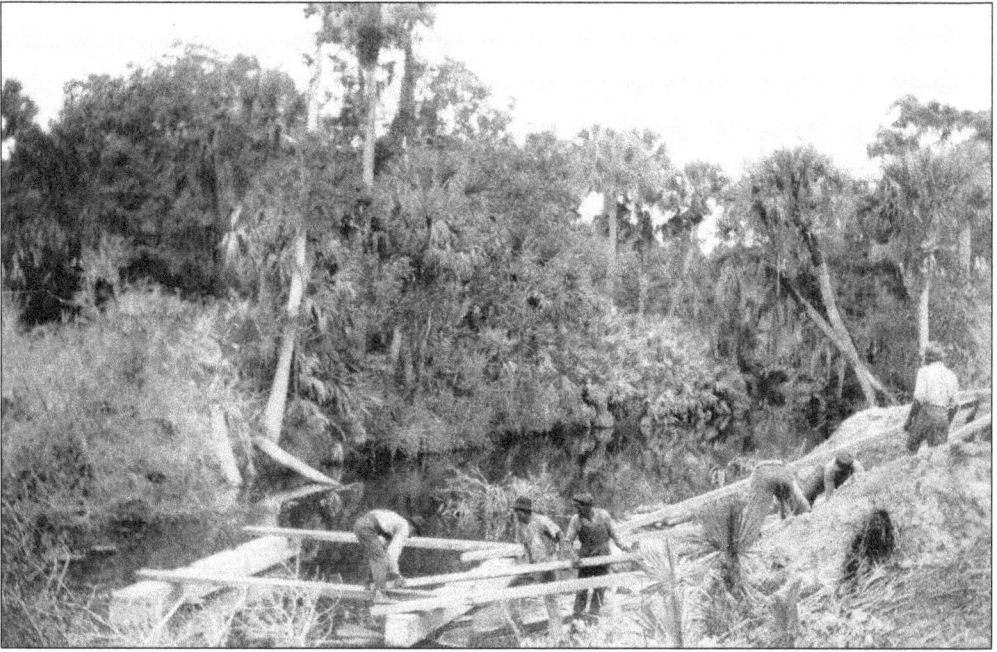

RAILROAD WORKERS. In 1910, ten African American laborers were employed by Fellsmere Farms Company to help construct the railroad and to cook for the survey party. Their numbers increased with the need for more laborers as the area added a packing plant, citrus groves, and farms. Primarily, African American settlers came to Fellsmere from other parts of Florida and from Georgia and South Carolina. (SIE.)

ST. SEBASTIAN RIVER BRIDGE. The bridge for the railroad track was completed sometime prior to 1911, the date the Fellsmere Farms Railroad commenced operations. Large dredges, excavators, ditchers, and other heavy equipment and supplies were hauled by train over this bridge to create the series of canals that was constructed to drain the Fellsmere area. (SIE.)

UNLOADING ARTESIAN WELL MACHINE. The Fellsmere Farms Company railroad was completed in 1911. It ran 9 miles from Fellsmere to the Sebastian station of the Florida East Coast Railroad and provided a transportation link for men and materials into Fellsmere. The artesian well equipment arrived by train to drill wells for the project. (SIE.)

BUCKEYE TRENCHER CROSSING THE RAILROAD TRACK. A new Buckeye trencher machine had to be ordered. The first ditcher that was brought in to Fellsmere to dig the canals was too heavy for the muck soil, and so the lighter trencher was ordered that could travel on the muck and cut narrow trenches. This would drain the ground sufficiently to support the larger ditcher equipment. (SIE.)

FELLSMERE DINKY TRAIN. The Dinky Train, a Model T Ford automobile, was modified with railroad wheels to run six days a week on the Fellsmere Railroad Company train track. It pulled one railroad car behind it and carried passengers, produce, and equipment. It took 45 minutes for the 9.94-mile trip and cost passengers 25¢. For large loads, a regular train engine was used. (IRCHS.)

MOTOR CAR ON THE FELLSMERE RAILROAD. The Fellsmere Railroad was incorporated in 1909. It began as the Sebastian and Cincinnatus Railroad. The floods of 1907–1908 caused Cincinnatus Farms to sell out. Fellsmere Farms Company took over and rebuilt it as the Fellsmere Railroad in 1910. In 1910–1911, the company ran a steam locomotive and a modified automobile on the tracks, pulling a passenger car, boxcar, and flatcars. (SIE.)

UNLOADING EQUIPMENT. By April 1912, Ernest H. Every, the Fellsmere manager in charge of the reclamation works of the Fellsmere tract, had built an extension of the railroad west of canal Lateral S to carry the equipment necessary to release surplus water from the northeast part of the township. Every's crews operated four excavators, three large dredges, and a Buckeye ditcher at that time, all brought in by train. (SIE.)

STRINGING TELEPHONE WIRE, FELLSMERE. A. A. Buck, general manager of Brevard Telephone Company, stated in his letter of October 18, 1913, to Ernest H. Every of Fellsmere Farms Company that a central telephone exchange would be installed and be in operation in Fellsmere by January, replacing the two-party lines owned and operated by Fellsmere Farms Company. Toll connections would be available to Sebastian over the Bell Telephone System. (SIE.)

OLD-STYLE WELL DRILL. The second artesian well on Fellsmere Farms Company land was drilled in January 1913 by Conkling Nursery Company and belonged to manager J. A. Martell. It was thought to be the strongest well sunk, drilled to 375 feet, flowing at 400 gallons per minute. Martell had a 2-acre grove of grapefruit, the first to be planted in the area at that time. (SIE.)

BONDHOLDER'S EXCURSION, AT LUNCH. In 1910, the board of directors for Fellsmere Farms Company first met, and a drainage proposal was obtained. In April 1911, promotion began. Dredging began in 1912. Brochures went out in 1913, and land sales commenced. Financing through mortgage bonds was obtained from the Columbia Trustee Company; however, title problems, a lawsuit, and the heavy flooding in 1915 forced the company into receivership by 1917. (SIE.)

DOMINIC M. DOMINICI. Dominici was a salesman for farms and groves property for Fellsmere Farms Company until he accepted a position with New York Life Insurance Company in 1915 and moved to West Palm Beach. In 1927, he moved back to Fellsmere and became a realtor selling land in Indian River and Brevard Counties again. (SIE.)

LAND BUYERS DOCKING. Sales agents were sent out by Fellsmere Farms Company into the north to locate prospective land buyers. Interested parties came by boat or by train. Persuasive sales techniques included refunds for the travel expenses, as little as $10 an acre for land purchase, and easy monthly payments. They came, they saw, they bought. (IRCHS-KOR.)

Six

FELLSMERE

TOWN OF FELLSMERE, DRY. Fellsmere Farms Company created two towns, Fellsmere and Broadmoor. Pictured is the Fellsmere town site before construction commenced in 1911. The *Fellsmere Farmer* newspaper announced February 21, 1912, that the town of Fellsmere was voted dry as to liquor use, and that not even a "blind tiger" would be allowed to prowl. It also announced that drainage of the land was assured. (SIE.)

BROADWAY, C. 1911–1912. On September 9, 1912, Olof Jonsson, at 72 years old, left St. Louis and walked 2,500 miles into Fellsmere, arriving in January 1913. He was short of funds and earned money along the way by repairing watches, clocks, and sewing machines, which netted him around $100. He said he would take another trip in order to accumulate a few hundred dollars more and come back to Fellsmere to start farming. (IRCHS.)

LOOKING NORTH ON BROADWAY STREET AT PENNSYLVANIA AVENUE. On the left is "The Bargain Store—General Merchandise." A block ahead on the left-hand side is the site of the Fellsmere Estates Corporation building and after that is the J. G. Carter store on the corner of Colorado Avenue. One block up on the right is the site of the future First Methodist Episcopal Church on the corner of Oregon Avenue. (SIE.)

BROADWAY, SOUTH. In 1913, electric lights were added to Broadway Street. Hall and Saunders decided to move their movie theater from the Workers of the World Hall into a new Dixie Playhouse building on Broadway Street that could seat 600. Brown Brothers Grocery Store took over the space formerly occupied by Vickers Brothers on that street. R. E. Brown was drawing up plans for a second store on Broadway that year. (KOR.)

MOORE'S DRUG STORE, FELLSMERE. In 1913, Dr. E. T. Moore, a horticulturist, bought a residence lot on Orange Street, where he constructed a bungalow for himself and his wife, Lucy. He also contracted with Walter Shupe to build his drugstore on the corner of New York Avenue and Broadway Street. Moore's Drug Store was open for business by the first of November 1913. (IRCHS.)

FELLSMERE BANK. The State Bank of Fellsmere opened for business July 1, 1913, in the one-story cream-colored brick building at the corner of Broadway Street and Colorado Avenue in Fellsmere. On the board of directors were Pres. Charles H. Piffard, first vice president Richard A. Conkling, second vice president Fred W. Kettle, E. Nelson Fell, and J. M. Bell. W. P. Dunn was cashier. (IRCHS.)

FELLSMERE SALES COMPANY OFFICE. William Drier, the director of sales at Fellsmere Sales Company, arrived with his wife and his entire office staff of nine on a Friday in January 1913 from Chattanooga, and he was permanently installed in the sales office on New York Avenue opposite the Farm House. They all spent their first day fishing at Lake Wilmington and familiarizing themselves with the area and then started work on Monday. (SIE.)

FELLSMERE ESTATES CORPORATION. Ammoniate Products Corporation adopted the Mission style of architecture for the distinctive design of its Fellsmere Estates Corporation building. It was erected around 1926 on north Broadway Street and served as its land sales office until it foreclosed in the 1930s. Since then, it has housed Florida Crystal Sugar Company headquarters, Fellsmere Police Department, and the city council, among others. It is now the popular Marsh Landing Restaurant. (SIE.)

FELLSMERE SCHOOL BEFORE RESTORATION. Fellsmere's first school, built in 1911, was a small woodframe structure. This brick building designed by architect Frederick H. Trimble was completed in 1916. In 1917, there were six in the graduating class: Mary Sale McCluer, Gwendolyn Hall, Mabel Bell, Audrey Claxton, Inez Dunnam, Hugh Roberts, and Joe Roberts. The school was restored in 2010 to house city hall and other civic facilities. (IRCHS.)

COMMUNITY CHURCH, FELLSMERE, C. 1913. On January 19, 1913, the members of the Fellsmere Farmers Fraternity met to establish a church for Fellsmere. Fellsmere Farms Company donated lots 10 through 17 of block 77, fronting on Hickory and Pennsylvania Streets for the church property, as well as a cash subscription of $500. Another 21 individuals pledged $625 toward the expected $2,000 total needed. (SIE.)

FIRST METHODIST EPISCOPAL CHURCH. This church was organized in 1914. The land was acquired in 1921 on north Broadway Street. The church is brick, in the Craftsman style of architecture, and was designed and built in 1924 by C. E. Nourse. The bell was obtained from the Daytona Community Methodist Church and installed in the belfry in 1924. This church is on the National Register of Historic Places. (IRCHS.)

MARIAN FELL LIBRARY, FELLSMERE. This library was created in 1915. Land was donated by Fellsmere Farms Company, and funds to erect the building were provided by Marian Fell from her work as a translator of Russian literature into English. The library was named in her honor by the Fellsmere Library Association. It is on the National Register of Historic Places. (IRCHS.)

FELLSMERE INN, C. 1925. In February 1912, the Fellsmere Inn was complete. It advertised reasonable rates, comfortable rooms, and excellent cuisine only two blocks from the Fellsmere Railway Station located on north Broadway Street. It was managed by R. G. Mills, and in 1913, it was sold to Theodore Moore of Miami. This inn was a social center for the community. It is on the National Register of Historic Places. (SIE.)

MANAGER'S HOUSE, WEST SIDE, FELLSMERE. Ernest H. Every, field manager for Fellsmere Farms Company, was born in England. Prior to coming to work for Fellsmere Farms Company, he had more than 20 years experience with irrigation projects in New Mexico and Colorado. He had been assistant manager of the U.S. Sugar and Land Company in Garden City, Kansas, as well. (SIE.)

BOARDINGHOUSE. Soon after her arrival in Fellsmere in 1912, Daisy Morris of Elk City, Oklahoma, responded to the great need for more temporary lodging. She purchased lots at Magnolia Street and New York Avenue to erect an eight-room, two-story private boardinghouse, artistically furnished, boasting a large veranda, and modern in every detail, including conveniences such as a bath. Awaiting its completion, she rented a small place for lodgers. (SIE.)

GEORGE KING HOUSE, FELLSMERE. This house was built around 1914 at the southeast corner of Pine Street and Idaho Avenue. Fellsmere residents were encouraged to name their homes, and George King named his *Green Gables*. It is a bungalow in the Craftsman style of architecture very popular at the time, and it is on the National Register of Historic Places. King served on the Fellsmere City Council for several years. (SIE.)

FELLSMERE BASEBALL, 1913. Throughout the 1912 and 1913 seasons, the Fellsmere team was most feared by East Coast clubs for its fast, aggressive style of play. Carl and Hugo Anderson and Ray "Little Mac" McDonald were brilliant players. The two games against the tough Fort Lauderdale team in August 1913 were considered the most important games of the season; almost the whole town of Fellsmere turned out to watch. (SIE.)

PACKING TOMATOES AT FELLSMERE. According to Richard A. Conkling, it was possible to grow 800 crates of tomatoes to the acre in Fellsmere soil. Dominic M. Dominici produced 1,600 crates on 8 acres in 1912. There were 150 railroad cars of tomatoes shipped north from the east coast of Florida in April 1912. In January 1913, it was estimated that 150 acres had been planted in tomatoes in Fellsmere Farms. (SIE.)

PLANTING SUGAR CANE, 1932. In order to produce sugar, 700 acres of Fellsmere land was cleared, prepared for planting, and fertilized. Seed cane had to be cut and planted, and the ground had to be rolled after planting. Systems of roadways and ditches were necessary. The planting of the first crop of Fellsmere Sugar Producers Company sugar cane was completed January 30, 1932. (SIE.)

FELLSMERE SUGAR MILL, SEPTEMBER 1, 1932. Construction on the sugar mill was completed in 1932. It was first thought that Frank W. Heiser would build his sugar mill on land east of Blue Cypress Lake, but he selected a site near Fellsmere instead. Processing of the sugar cane crops began in 1933. (SIE.)

MOLASSES TANKS AWAITING SHIPMENT. The acres of sugar cane planted in the Fellsmere area brought the sugar mills and refineries. One of their products was molasses, shipped out in the mid-1930s by rail, filling as many as 20 tank cars at a time. The Trans Florida Central Railroad between Fellsmere and Sebastian carried the tank cars to the Florida East Coast Railway interchange at Sebastian to be shipped north. (SIE.)

STEAM ENGINE, BOXCAR, AND PASSENGER CAR AT FELLSMERE. The passenger terminal at Fellsmere for the Fellsmere railroad was completed in 1913 on the north side of South Carolina Avenue at Broadway Street. Thus passengers disembarked right at the main thoroughfare of downtown Fellsmere. Passenger business was so brisk at the height of the land-sales boom for Fellsmere Farms Company that two larger passenger coaches were added. (SIE.)

LOCOMOTIVE NO. 101 AT THE MUCK PLANT, C. 1924. Renovations and improvements on the rail lines began in September 1923 to enable the track to haul heavier loads. Locomotive No. 101 was then used to haul the cars of peat deposits from the muck around Broadmoor to Fellsmere for processing. At the plant in Fellsmere, it was dried and shipped to Sebastian and then on north in boxcars as fertilizer. (SIE.)

Seven

WABASSO

U.S. HIGHWAY 1 WABASSO. Pioneers began settling in the Wabasso area around the turn of the century, planting crops and groves. George Sears and Tom Cail were among the first. In May 1915, it was announced that a new national highway would be created, the Dixie National Highway. It would run from Chicago to Miami along the Florida east coast. By 1917, the Wabasso section had been completed. (VAN.)

WABASSO LOOKING EAST, C. 1914. The building on the right is the general store that was owned by Elmer. E. Smith. The residences on the left belong to, from left to right, Adam Eby, Sam Beer, Elmer E. Smith, George Sears, and Tom Cail. The photograph was taken by Sigsby Scruggs who was a teacher at Wabasso Elementary School at that time. He climbed a tree to take this picture. (IRCHS.)

ELMER E. SMITH'S STORE, WABASSO, 1909. Elmer E. Smith and his family moved to Wabasso in 1904, and soon thereafter he bought the general store from a Mr. Conklin. The post office for Wabasso was located in his store. Seminole Indians often traded here with Smith. The Smiths' home was across the street from the store, four houses down. The photograph was taken by John Cates. (VAN.)

70

MILDRED SMITH, WABASSO, 1910. Mildred Smith, on the farthest right, is seated next to Clarence Vandiveer with Jacob O. Jameson, Irene Smith, and Ginger Pearl Holt. She lived with her parents, Elmer and Dora, at their home *Ridgewood* in Wabasso until her marriage in November 1923 to Horace Henry Gifford of Vero. She died only five years later, in 1927. Horace Gifford was part owner of Florida Sporting Goods Company. (IRCHS.)

WABASSO SCHOOL, BUILT IN 1925. When Elmer E. Smith arrived in Wabasso in 1904 with five daughters, a dozen people started applauding, because now they had enough children to qualify for a school. On November 5, 1905, a notice was placed in the paper that the Wabasso public school, a wooden-frame building, was now open. In 1925, this new brick, two-story school was completed for $30,000. (IRCHS.)

PICNIC NEAR THE ELMER E. SMITH HOUSE, WABASSO, C. 1910. Seated second from the left at the back table is John Edmund Jameson with white hair, and seated farthest right is his wife, Katherine Greybill Jameson, with white hair. They were the parents of Olive, Jay O., and Thad Jameson, and in 1910, the parents resided in Juniata, Fayette County, Pennsylvania. The Greybill family lived nearby in Pennsylvania. (IRCHS.)

SMITH FAMILY POSING BY THE FAMILY CAR, EARLY 1900s. The entire Smith family was dressed up for this photograph. From left to right are (first row) daughters Florence R., Marion, little Elizabeth J. in front of Elmer E. Smith, son David C. "Bo" Smith in front of daughter Olive K., and mother Dora M. Smith on the far right; (second row) daughters Mildred and Irene. (IRCHS.)

TAKING A RIDE, WABASSO, C. 1910. Taking a ride in their Sunday finery are, from left to right, Irene Smith, Pearl Hale, unidentified, D. K. Jameson, Mildred Smith in the white dress, Clarence Vandiveer, and Jacob O. Jameson on the horse. J. O. was a pastor of the Methodist Episcopal church in Wabasso in the 1920s. In 1923, he was also responsible for the erection of a parsonage. (IRCHS.)

GRACE UNITED METHODIST CHURCH, WABASSO, C. 1930. In March 1917, the Methodist church was formally organized, and the members elected to build a church. Although several others offered, the property donated for the church by Laura Vandiveer was accepted, as it was most centrally located. Charles Cook, an architect, volunteered to design it. Work was begun under the supervision of Jacob O. Jameson and Charles Vandiveer and completed that same year. (IRCHS.)

73

ARTHUR AND LAURA VANDIVEER, WABASSO, 1906. Arthur was born in Miamisburg, Ohio, and came to Wabasso in 1908 with his family. Travel from Ohio to Florida involved several changes of trains and a steamboat trip and took almost two days including stops. They are standing on their homesite in Wabasso where U.S. Highway 1 is today, in front of the Methodist church. (VAN.)

VANDIVEER HOUSE, WABASSO. From 1910 until the 1960s, the Vandiveer house, which is no longer in existence, stood across the street from the Methodist church in Wabasso, west of U.S. Highway 1. Arthur W. Vandiveer and his wife, Laura Groby Vandiveer, moved to Wabasso for reasons of health with their children Charles P., Clarence A., and Allie. Arthur was in the tobacco business in Ohio. (VAN.)

CHARLES VANDIVEER'S FIRST HOME. Charles Vandiveer; his wife, Bessie; and children Hazel and Robert all moved to Wabasso from Ohio with his parents. He used his skills as a carpenter to build a home for his family located next to the home occupied by his parents, Arthur and Laura, and brother Clarence. This one was noted for its water tank, seen at the side. (VAN.)

CHARLES VANDIVEER'S SECOND HOUSE. Charles Pearson Vandiveer continued to use his carpentry skills building this house. He also oversaw the construction of the Wabasso School, stepping in after Jacob O. Jameson began the construction on August 13, 1917, on the lot donated from the Vandiveer estate by Laura Vandiveer. (VAN.)

CLARENCE A. VANDIVEER, WORLD WAR I. According to his discharge certificate, Clarence Vandiveer was a private in the St. Lucie County Home Guard during World War I. He enlisted July 5, 1918, to serve for three years, but the whole company was mustered out July 7, 1919. He was 5 feet, 6 inches tall and weighed 140 pounds. His occupation was listed as farmer. His character and service were both first class. (VAN.)

CLARENCE VANDIVEER AND OLIVE JAMESON, SEATED. Olive moved from McAllisterville, Pennsylvania, to Wabasso as a mother's helper to the Elmer E. Smith family in 1904. She married John H. Longaker in 1913 on the condition that he agree to live in Florida. They purchased 18 acres and built a two-story house next to her brother's house a quarter mile north of the Wabasso crossroads. (VAN.)

R. W. JAMESON HOUSE, WABASSO, C. 1936. This house, built around 1921, still stands on U.S. Highway 1 in Wabasso. Lottie and R. W. Jameson were residents of McAlisterville, Pennsylvania, prior to moving to Wabasso in 1919. Their son James R. Jameson was vice president and treasurer of Deerfield Groves Company in Wabasso. He was slated to become president of Deerfield but died suddenly on a trip before it could take place. (IRCHS.)

POWERS RESIDENCE. The Powers house was built on the Dixie Highway at Wabasso about 1921–1922 and still remains there. J. L. Powers was a citrus grower, school teacher, and superintendent of public instruction. Powers became the first mayor of the City of Wabasso when it incorporated in November 1925. The office of the American Fruit Growers Association was used as the city hall. (VAN.)

WILLIAM A. EARLY. William married Allie Vandiveer in 1892 in Dayton, Ohio. After Clarence Vandiveer came to Wabasso in 1907, he persuaded the rest of the family to move there in 1908. William and Allie Early also came to Wabasso at Clarence's urging and built a cottage there. They spent their winters there until William's death in 1932, at which time Allie moved permanently to Wabasso. (VAN.)

THE EARLY HOME. Pictured are Allie and William Early in front of their home. The home was located on the east side of Dixie Highway on the road that led to the old wooden Wabasso Bridge. The road was lined with Australian pines planted by the Works Progress Administration. William Barker worked for the Works Progress Administration and helped plant the trees. (VAN.)

WABASSO BRIDGE. It was quite an adventure to use the first Wabasso Bridge. Rain made the surface very slick, and more than one truck slid through the railings into the river. Also, the bridge was wooden and prone to fires. Ledges were built along the sides to hold buckets for water. Drivers were expected to douse any fires and alert the bridge tender. One bridge tender shot at speeders. (IRCHS.)

A PICNIC ON THE BEACH. Before there were bridges, local travel to and from the beach had to be by boat. Here the Vandiveers and Earlys got together with friends to go to the beach after church. Travel for both commerce and pleasure was eased by the erection of the Vero bridge in 1920, the Winter Beach bridge in 1927, and the Wabasso Bridge in 1927. (VAN.)

HOME OF DAVID AND SADIE WISE. The Wise home was across U.S. Highway 1 from the Arthur Snyder Sr. house in Wabasso. Shown are, from left to right, Irene Wise, Arthur Snyder Sr., and Elma Snyder Wise. In 1917–1918, David Wise contributed a considerable portion of the construction work on the new church near his home. (VAN.)

HAZEL SKINNER'S HOUSE, MARCH 31, 1929. Arthur M. Snyder Sr. built this home on Old Dixie Highway, where the Publix store now stands, across the street from his mother and stepfather, David and Sadie Wise. After he died from a ruptured appendix, his wife, Hazel Vandiveer Snyder, remarried to B. C. Skinner and lived in this house until she passed away. Her son sold it after she died. (VAN.)

ARTHUR SNYDER SR. WITH HIS TRUCK. Arthur M. Snyder Sr. lived with his wife, Hazel, in this house on U. S. Highway 1 in Wabasso until his death in 1929. He was a fruit hauler for the American Fruit Grower's Association. In World War I, he was a private in the 155th Depot Brigade. (VAN.)

TROOP NO. 1, WABASSO BOY SCOUTS OF AMERICA, 1934. Scouts shown are, from left to right, (seated) John Aughtman, Raymond Beers, Michael McDonald, William James, Dorsey Roddenberg, and Harvey Beers; (standing) Samuel Beers, David Cathcard, Jacob O. Jameson, and Howard O'Steen. Boy Scout and Girl Scout troops hosted joint suppers at the beach, and Boy Scouts held parent night suppers at the Wabasso School. (IRCHS.)

C&W Service Station at Wabasso. After his arrival in 1922, Thomas R. Cadenhead opened a store and filling station with C. B. Osteen in Wabasso. His wife, Dorothy Cadenhead, operated the Cozy Café next door to the filling station across Dixie Highway from the school. In 1927, over by the railroad tracks, he opened the Wabasso Mercantile Company with L. B. O'Steen and Mary Whittington. (IRCHS.)

Wabasso Train Wreck, 1917. On January 7, 1917, a freight train wrecked during the night, and seven freight cars were demolished. It took seven days for the wrecking crew sent from the north to clear away the wreckage and repair the damage. (VAN.)

HELPLING'S SERVICE STATION, U.S. HIGHWAY 1, WABASSO. Junior Lawrence Helpling, son of Oscar and Elsie Helpling of Wabasso, was a county commissioner. He was married to Jean Powers, a neighbor on U.S. Highway 1. He died of an illness at the early age of 45, in 1949. Pictured is Helpling's service station. It was sold to John and Robert Longacre in 1940. (IRCHS.)

THE "FROGROTTO FISH," WABASSO, 1930s. Behind Oscar Helpling's log cabin house on U.S. Highway 1 was a large stone structure shaped like a jug with goldfish and water hyacinths. It had a mill wheel cascade of water over a walkway and another pool with more goldfish. Farther back was a canal with 3,000 frogs available for fishing. He called these attractions the "Frogrottofish" and "Jugofisch." (IRCHS.)

GRAVES BROTHERS SAWMILL, WABASSO. Arriving in Florida in the late 1800s, brothers J. Edwin Graves and Walter F. Graves purchased timber rights to 30,000 acres west of Indian River Farms. This acreage extended from a half-mile north of State Road 60 nearly to the Fleming Grant. They erected a sawmill west of the railroad tracks in Wabasso. The original Wabasso Bridge was built with their lumber. (IRCHS.)

JACOB AND THAD JAMESON PACKING FRUIT, WABASSO, 1913. Standing is Jacob O. Jameson, and seated is Thad Jameson. The Graves brothers built their first fruit and vegetable packinghouse in Wabasso. One of the first trademarks they obtained was a stylized mark "Selco," first used in 1922 for fresh or raw citrus fruits, tomatoes, cucumbers, peppers, and potatoes. These businessmen grew vegetables and owned groves, timber, a sawmill, and packinghouses. (IRCHS.)

Eight

INDIAN RIVER FARMS COMPANY

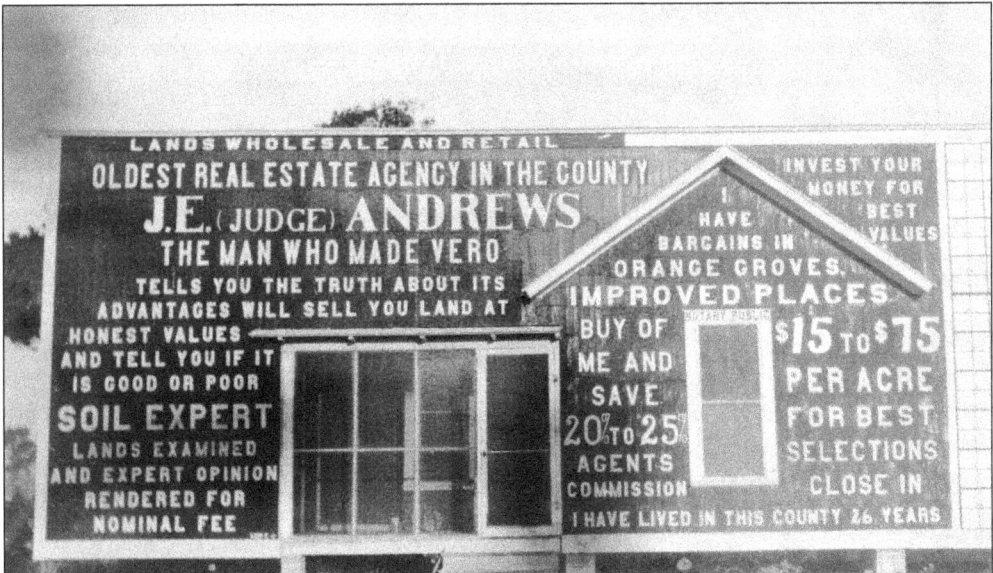

ANDREWS ADVERTISING BILLBOARD. County judge James E. Andrews was an enthusiastic supporter of the possibilities for growth in this area. In 1912, Judge Andrews was instrumental in the sale of the 55,000 acres of land that formed the Indian River Farms Company development, and he was the company's first manager. He encouraged William Atkin to organize and open the Farmer's Bank, and Judge Andrews was its first president. (TY.)

SMALL DITCH DIGGER, LATERAL 1. The C. M. Rogers and Company engineering firm was hired by Herman Zeuch to conduct a feasibility study for converting the Vero marshland into farmland. A crew of 12 surveyors and engineers arrived in January 1912 led by Robert Daniel Carter. Draglines, dipper dredges, and large and small ditchers created the canals. Everyone lived in tents on whatever high ground they could find. (TY.)

MAIN CANAL OUTLET TO THE INDIAN RIVER. Before surveying for canals and lots could commence, it was necessary to complete the surveying of the section and quarter-section lines that were never finished by the federal government. Where Robert Carter's surveyors worked, the water was as much as 2 feet deep. The mules were spooked by fish swimming around under their bellies. The men and animals were plagued by mosquitoes and horseflies. (TY.)

PALM TREE OVERLOOKING THE NORTH RELIEF CANAL, 1920. The North Relief Canal ran 5 miles from the Indian River to the Range Line Canal. The extensive system of canals and laterals took 17 years to design and complete. A catch basin was created to stop sediment from the canal from entering the Indian River. C. R. Cummins and Company was in charge of the excavation. (IRCHS.)

SLEEPY EYE DINING ROOM, C. 1912–1917. Leslie J. Daly of Carter and Damerow is at the front left table in the black suit. The Mahers are at the front table on the right in the new Sleepy Eye dining room. The dining room was a small building erected adjacent to the Sleepy Eye Lodge to accommodate the constant influx of prospective buyers inspecting the Indian River Farms Company land. (TY.)

WHY NOT LIVE

Where outdoor life, so conducive to health, is possible the year around.

"Where something can be grown and marketed every month in the year."

Join one of our twice-a-month excursions and personally inspect INDIAN RIVER FARMS and see for yourself why Indian River Farms is the best proposition in Florida, whether you want a large or small tract for fruit growing, trucking, general farming or cattle, hog or poultry raising. Write us for details.

INDIAN RIVER FARMS COMPANY, Vero, Fla.

INDIAN RIVER FARMS COMPANY ADVERTISING CARD. Cards, postcards, and newspapers were continuously sent north extolling the worth of purchasing their land. The *Indian River Farmer* was a newspaper published by Indian River Farms Company. Progress on the drainage canals, new commercial establishments, successful farms, crop yields, and social news of new arrivals were touted in this paper, which was most likely published from 1912 to the early 1920s. (SMI.)

POTENTIAL CUSTOMERS. Specially scheduled trains with reduced fares brought in large groups to see the land on each run. The groups were housed at the Sleepy Eye Lodge or one of the rooming houses. Cavalcades of cars with a salesman took them to see some of the prosperous farms already established, such as the demonstration farm, Eli Walker's groves, or James J. Roberts's groves. (IRCHS.)

PROSPECTIVE BUYERS. In November 1913, Waldo Sexton brought Spaulding tilling equipment to Vero to demonstrate for Indian River Farms Company. He became so enthralled with the Indian River Farms Company property development project that he became a spokesman for that company instead. Large numbers of interested individuals arrived every day for a tour of the area. The Sleepy Eye Lodge on Fourteenth Avenue is at the left. (SX.)

WALDO SEXTON'S DEMONSTRATION. The handwriting on the face of this picture is Waldo Sexton's. On the reverse side he wrote, "This was on Osceola Boulevard between Maher's Department Store and Ann's Tavern. I was giving demonstration of the Spaulding Tilling Machine. Tony Young at the wheel; A. M. Hill, photographer." Sexton's second job after graduating from Purdue University in 1911 was for the Spalding Deep Tilling Machine Company. (SX.)

nov. 1914

SLEEPY EYE LODGE, VERO. This hotel was erected by James Hudson Baker around 1913 at Fourteenth Avenue and Twenty-first Street to house the prospective buyers of the Indian River Farms Company land. First named Bayhead Inn, it was soon renamed the Sleepy Eye Lodge, in honor of a Minnesota Indian chief. In the 1920s, it was moved to make room for the Del Mar Hotel and renamed the Del Prado. (IRCHS.)

ROOMS FOR RENT, VERO. The constant influx of prospective land buyers filled boomtown Vero to capacity. Twitchell's Pool Hall on Twentieth Street in downtown Vero was the first commercial establishment erected with rooms to let over the pool hall. The Sleepy Eye Lodge was built in 1912. In the 1916 directory are two other establishments with rooms, Martha E. Knight's and Emma Trice's. (IRCHS.)

FULFILLING THE INDIAN RIVER DREAM. This could be the start of an "ideal 40-acre farm" promised by Indian River Farms Company advertising flyers and postcards from about 1912–1920s. First build the spacious farmhouse; then borrow a horse and plow; sow the vegetable crop; get the artesian well drilled; plant the citrus grove, sugar cane, and pineapples; buy the chickens, cows and hogs; and build the barns and sheds. (IRCHS.)

HOME OF HENRY RIDENOUR. This is one of the first houses built on Indian River Farms Company land, which was erected in June 1913 on Lateral A Road (Sixty-sixth Avenue), a half mile south of Winter Beach Road. Henry and his wife, Blanche Ridenour, were originally from Colorado and spent one summer there after moving to Vero. Prof. Myron E. Hard started building his home at the same time as the Ridenours. (MAC.)

REBECCA AND MOTHER MARY RODENBERG. The Rodenberg family arrived in Vero about 1915, attracted to the area by a picture in a church magazine. Mary C. Rodenberg was a schoolteacher and the wife of Frank W. Rodenberg, who was a Vero postmaster, a Methodist supply minister, and a Mason. They had two children, a son Henry and a daughter Edith Rebecca Rodenberg. Edith was also a teacher and never married. (IRCHS.)

ANTHONY W. YOUNG. Anthony arrived in Vero in 1912 and became sales manager of Indian River Farms Company. Growing Sea Island cotton was one of his pursuits. His varied credits included service in army intelligence in World War I, first mayor of Vero, member of the Florida Citrus Control Committee, and state senator. His strong civic presence helped develop Vero and Indian River County. (TY.)

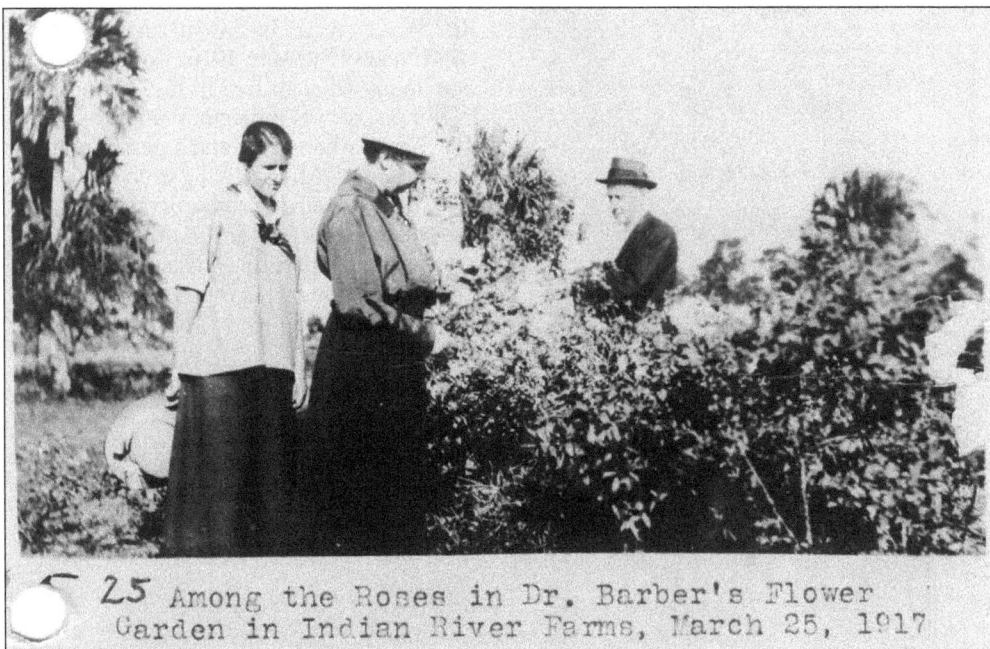

25 Among the Roses in Dr. Barber's Flower
Garden in Indian River Farms, March 25, 1917

DR. BARBER'S FLOWER GARDEN, 1917. This photograph was on one of the many postcards sent out to advertise the excellent quality of life to be found on Indian River Farms Company land. Dr. Merrill J. Barber moved to Vero in 1913 with his wife and three-year-old son Merrill P. Barber. He was one of the first citrus growers in the area, and his wife's rose garden was famous. (IRCHS.)

PART OF DIXIE HIGHWAY THREE YEARS AFTER TREES WERE SET, 1917. Even the Dixie Highway was used as a selling point by Indian River Farms Company; neat, accessible highways were now running through Florida, dispelling the myth of an impenetrable wilderness. However, when Anna H. Chamberlain traveled by car from Fort Pierce to DeLand in June 1919, she suffered four flat tires during the 14-hour trip (roughly 150 miles). (IRCHS.)

ROY WAKER AND HIS SAWMILL MULES IN THE CYPRESS SWAMPS, 1916. Roy Waker wore many different hats in his lifetime. In Illinois, he was inspector/manager for the Glen Carbon Mine and a professional photographer. After arriving in Vero in 1914, he continued as a photographer, became a commercial citrus grove owner, a farmer, and a part-time logger. He and his brother were owners and operators of the Seminole Grocery. (IRCHS.)

WAKER HOMESTEAD, MARCH 1917. On the left is Aunt Mary from Collinsville, Illinois, and Irene Waker is at the pump. The Waker home had both regular well water and artesian well water. The regular well water was full of minerals and stained everything yellow. They drank the artesian well water, believing it to be healthier, although the water was very hard. They had a generator for electricity. (IRCHS.)

94

CLEARING THE WAKER LAND, 1915. Oxen were used by Louis Waker (on the left), father of Roy Waker, and Sam Smith, to clear the 10 acres of land purchased by Roy Waker on Eighth Street south of Twenty-second Avenue in Vero. After clearing, it was planted in citrus trees, with a cash crop of truck garden vegetables in between the rows. (IRCHS.)

ELIZABETH "LIZZIE" LEFFLER (CENTER). In 1914, Elizabeth and her husband, Peter Leffler, moved to Vero from Glen Carbon, Illinois. Elizabeth suffered from lung ailments in 1921 and spent two months in Homestead, Florida, seeking medical treatment. Although completely cured in 1921, she died in 1924 at age 36 from further lung trouble. (IRCHS.)

Winter Potatoes grown in Indian River Farms; planted
in February and marketed the early part of May, 1917.
These are the kind of potatoes that brought $9.00 per
barrel, f.o.b. Vero.

WINTER POTATOES. A selling point for Indian River Farms Company was that farmers could easily grow large quantities of fresh vegetables in the winter. In 1920, state agent C. K. McQuarrie warned that Florida farmers were producing too many varieties of potatoes, preventing standardization of the crop for shipment north. Vero had 500 acres planted in potatoes that year, making it the leading producer in the county. (IRCHS.)

A FIELD OF SUDAN GRASS. Another selling point for Indian River Farms Company was that the soil was ideal for growing all of the best pasture grasses, such as Sudan grass, Napier, Merker, Johnson, Para grasses, and sorghum and cowpeas. Grasses grown and exhibited at the county fairs included Natal grass, Rhodes, Para, Sudan, Bermuda, St. Augustine, Carab, Crab Grass, German Millet, Boggar West, and Cattail Millet. (IRCHS.)

Nine

VERO BEACH

GIFFORD STORE AND POST OFFICE. Built in 1898 by Henry Gifford, this store and post office faced the Gifford home on what was later to become Osceola Boulevard in Vero. Henry and his daughter arrived in the area in the 1880s, advised to move south for his health. The rest of his family arrived in 1888. He was appointed the first postmaster in Vero in 1891. (IRCHS.)

LIBERTY PARK, VERO. Liberty Park, foreground, was adjacent to the Sleepy Eye Lodge on Fourteenth Avenue, seen here back left. They no longer exist. The first anniversary of Armistice Day was celebrated in Liberty Park, November 15, 1919. An estimated 3,000 people came to celebrate in downtown Vero. One prize offered was a free city lot of land, won by Albert B. Bates. (TY.)

TWENTIETH STREET AT FOURTEENTH AVENUE LOOKING NORTH, VERO, C. 1916. In this early street scene, the Farmer's Bank, prior to its face-lift, is seen on the corner. The automobiles are parked in front of tenants of this building, the Vero Drug Company owned by Chuck McClure and the post office. Campbell's Barber Shop is around the corner on the left. (IRCHS.)

FOURTH OF JULY CELEBRATION, VERO. Everyone is dressed up, ready to celebrate. The parade is beginning to form on Twentieth Street at Fourteenth Avenue in downtown Vero. The sign on the parade car proudly proclaims, "4th of July Celebration." Cars not in the parade are parked in front of Jun's Grocery, Twitchell's Pool Hall with rooms for rent on the second floor, and Maher's Department Store. (IRCHS.)

AERIAL VIEW VERO BEACH. In the back, center, are the trees of Pocahontas Park. Next on the right is the Seminole Building on the corner of Fourteenth Avenue and Twenty-first Street. On the far right can be seen the vertical sign of the Vero Theatre. Across the street from the Seminole Building is the front lawn of the Vero Del Mar Hotel. In the center stands a café. (IRCHS.)

TWENTIETH STREET BETWEEN FOURTEENTH AND FIFTEENTH AVENUES, VERO. From left to right are Frinks Store(?), the Vero Drug Company, U.S. Post Office, Army Store, J. P. Skinners(?), and Vero Press. None of these buildings remain. On September 18, 1919, the first copy of the *Vero Press* was printed. On April 24, 1923, the *Vero Press* moved into its new building on Twenty-first Street. It became the *Vero Beach Press* in June 1925. (IRCHS.)

AERIAL VIEW, TWENTIETH STREET AT FIFTEENTH AVENUE, VERO BEACH, 1926. Osceola Apartments is at 1510 Twentieth Street on the left. Fiske and Sell Service Station is across the street from it, with Vero Beach Auto Park to the right. Vero Del Mar Hotel is in the far right background. The little building in front of it is Merriman Real Estate, which was later moved to Main Street. (IRCHS.)

COMMERCE AVENUE, VERO, 1917. These high-wheeled oxen carts were ideal for the area's soft, marshy land. The train depot is on the left. On the right is Jimmy Knight's General Store and the icehouse operated by his brother Redden Knight. Redden also built a bottling plant and made the popular soft drink Grape-Ade. Jimmy was postmaster from 1911 to 1914 and had a Standard Oil distributorship as well. (IRCHS.)

DIXIE HIGHWAY, VERO. This photograph was taken by Rudolph Herman Cassens. The Edgewood Hotel, on the left, was built on Dixie Highway in 1917 and moved to Seminole Avenue in 1923. The side of Farmer's Bank can be seen at the end of the street; James A. Frere's lumberyard is on the right, marked with an "X" by a family member. (OGU.)

THE SEMINOLE BUILDING, 1918. Vero grew rapidly during this time. The streets and sidewalks were paved, and commerce was booming. Construction was nearly finished on the Seminole Building, shown here prior to its completion in July 1918, by builders Wolf and Ewing. Early tenants were the Seminole Grocery and Simmons Dry Goods Store. It faced the Sleepy Eye Lodge, seen on the right. (TY.)

ROACH GARAGE 1912, OLD DIXIE HIGHWAY AND TWENTIETH STREET. Ottaway Roach moved to Vero in 1901 and was the first person to buy land, 5 acres for $75, from Henry Gifford. Roach built the first garage where he kept the only radio in town. People congregated there to listen to the games. In 1923, this became the fire station, housing the fire truck, and Roach became the first fire chief. (IRCHS.)

JUN'S MARKET. Thomas Jun's market was built on Osceola Boulevard in Vero in 1919 and opened in June 1920. He ran it until he retired in 1944. Jun's Cash and Carry Grocery advertised prompt service, a square deal, service satisfaction, a clean store, clean stock, and quality groceries. He was known for his unique and tempting window displays that had to be seen to be appreciated. (IRCHS.)

OSCEOLA BOULEVARD BEFORE THE FIRE. In November 1919, a fire destroyed the entire block of Osceola Boulevard (Twentieth Street) between Fourteenth and Fifteenth Avenues. It burned to the ground with very little furnishings saved. From west to east, the shops that burned were Mrs. Trice's hotel, Victory Restaurant, Twitchell's poolroom and barbershop, Maher's Department Store, and Allison Brothers Grocery and Market. By December 18, they began rebuilding. (IRCHS.)

VERO CITY HALL AND THE BEINDORF BOYS, 1923. In 1921, William C. Beindorf and his son Paul A. Beindorf decided to move their machine shop from Litchfield, Illinois, to Vero. In 1922, the machinery was packed up and moved to Vero, and the Vero Machine and Supply Shop opened that same year on Dixie Highway near Seventeenth Street. It manufactured attachments for Ford cars and trucks, the "Suhl Six-Wheeler." (IRCHS.)

FISKE AND SELL SERVICE STATION, 1926. The Fiske and Sell Service Station opened in August 1926 at Twentieth Street and Fifteenth Avenue, Vero Beach, with the slogan, "Service that is Different," promising superior service and supplies. By October 1926, G. L. Fiske and Lee C. Sell dissolved their partnership, and it became the Sell Service Station. It was purchased by Sinclair Oil in 1929. (SEL.)

PHOTOGRAPHED AT VERO BEACH ELEMENTARY SCHOOL BEFORE 1926. Shown are, from left to right, (first row) both unidentified; (second row) Dorothy Hennig, Florence Leffler, Anne Gollnick, Irene Sheffield, two unidentifieds, Alice Palmer of Wabasso, unidentified, and Bethany Routh; (third row) Hugh Poole, Ms. Dubose, and Paul Robertson. (IRCHS.)

NEW VERO SCHOOL BUS. In September 1919, Vero's new school opened. Its first school bus driver, Leon B. Gollnick, had the contract for transporting children throughout the district to school. He purchased a new Oldsmobile truck and added a body with a seating capacity of 35 with seats on each side and down the middle. Either Leon or his wife, Lillie, drove the bus each day. (IRCHS.)

BAPTIST CHURCH, VERO, C. 1914. Looking north on Sixteenth Avenue between Twenty-first and Twenty-second Streets, the First Baptist Church is on the right, and the left extreme foreground is the present-day site of the Indian River County Main Library and rear parking lot. When the main library moved to this area, it displaced several houses and the Grace Lutheran Church on Seventeenth Avenue. (PMM.)

ST. HELEN'S CATHOLIC CHURCH, VERO. This wood-frame church was built in 1919 at the corner of Twenty-first Street and Twentieth Avenue, made possible by a donation from the Catholic Extension Society of Chicago. Prior to 1919, parishioners had to travel to Fort Pierce to celebrate Mass. Rev. Rupert Gabriel was its first pastor. A resident of Fort Pierce, he was responsible for parishes from Rockledge to Okeechobee. (IRCHS.)

WOMAN'S CLUB, C. 1917. This photograph is a familiar sight. It shows the Vero Beach Woman's Club, still in existence at 1534 Twenty-first Street. However, originally it was named the Myron E. Hard Memorial Library, in honor Professor Hard, an author who was a noted and respected member of the Vero community for the short time he lived there. He arrived in August 1914 and died three months later. (IRCHS.)

VERO TRAIN DEPOT, 1914. The Vero depot is shown here on Commerce Avenue prior to renovations when it was converted from a freight depot to a passenger depot. The depot was enlarged by placing siding between the exposed posts. Commerce Avenue is seen to the left, with an automobile by Knight's General Store. The depot was moved to its current location at Fourteenth Avenue and Twenty-third Street. (IRCHS.)

READY FOR A SPIN, 1918. Pictured here are Maude Waker and Robert Harris in his "Tin Lizzie." Waker came to Vero by train from Illinois in 1915. She was a store clerk and played the piano at the movie house. She never married, although she was courted by both Eli Walker after his divorce and by Robert Harris, a World War I serviceman stationed in Key West. (IRCHS.)

FASHIONABLE VERO JUNE BRIDE, 1923. Frida Klingsick and James Burrell Tippin Sr. were married June 17, 1923, at Grace Lutheran Church. Frida wore a dress of Canton crepe and a veil worn by 15 women before her. This pioneer couple from Missouri honeymooned in Tampa, New Orleans, and St. Louis, traveling by boat. Titling himself the "Sage of the Sawgrass," James wrote letters and essays about Florida. (TIP.)

FRANK J. FRANEK, WORLD WAR I, AN
ABRIDGED LETTER HOME, NOVEMBER 14,
1918. "Dear Sis: Your letter of November 3rd
received Friday. Lot of men seem to think we
will be on our way home before the year is
out. I only hope so. I will be glad to get myself
back in the states. What do the girls want me
to bring them? As ever. Frank." (IRCHS.)

VERO WAR EFFORT. These auto mechanics put their skills to good use. During World War I, these
three young men helped the Red Cross recycle automobile tires for the war effort in Vero. From
left to right are Tobias Sebastian Gobar, Chris Bell, and Joseph Early Twitchell. Gobar was a self-
employed auto mechanic, and Twitchell was a garage owner and city mechanic. (IRCHS.)

BAKER HOUSE, FIFTEENTH AVENUE AND NINETEENTH STREET, VERO 1913. James Hudson Baker, brother-in-law of Mrs. Trice, was the first person to be roused when a block of Osceola Boulevard in downtown Vero caught fire in 1919. Baker was a building contractor who arrived in Vero with his family in 1912 and was responsible for construction of many local homes and commercial buildings. He is on the Great Floridians List. (IRCHS.)

ELI C. WALKER RESIDENCE, FIFTY-EIGHTH AVENUE, VERO. Pioneer citrus grower and civic leader Eli C. Walker began as a storekeeper and postmaster. Following his arrival in the late 1890s, he purchased and planted approximately 400 acres in citrus. He served on the board of county commissioners and was a supervisor of the Indian River Farms Drainage District. In 1934, he became a representative in the Florida State Legislature. (IRCHS.)

GEORGE THOMAS TIPPIN HOUSE, CLEMMONS AVENUE, VERO, C. 1916. This typical Vero home was owned by pioneer Tippin, born in Greenbriar, Indiana. Vero became his home in 1910. A man of many abilities, he was a philosopher, the published author of *Man, Metal and Money*, an agriculture specialist, secretary of the chamber of commerce, and the county supervisor of registration of voters, during his long career. (TIP.)

NISLE HOUSE. Paul H. Nisle was a local pioneer who moved to Vero in 1919 and founded the *Vero Press* newspaper during that same year. He was also the first prosecuting attorney for Indian River County. This house was built soon after his arrival at 2051 Sixteenth Avenue (current location of the courthouse parking garage) in Vero and was renovated in 1922 with a five-room addition. (NIS.)

LILLIE ANTHONY'S HOME. In 1920, Lillie Anthony had a six-room bungalow built for her by T. S. Rodenberry on one of her lots east of the railroad. This was enlarged in 1926. She moved to new lodgings in 1937 on Tenth Avenue. She was postmistress, and at one time she managed the Cozy Café. A Daughters of the American Revolution member and family genealogist, she never married. (IRCHS.)

BOATING PARTY, DR. GROSSMAN'S LAUNCH. In 1916, Dr. Frederick Grossman moved his office from his home to rooms over Maher's Dry Goods Store in Vero. C. W. Riggs constructed a new residence for him in 1921, two stories and 12 rooms in tile and stucco, on Osceola Boulevard. Cox Funeral Home took over that building in 1934. It is still in existence. (IRCHS.)

VERO BASKETBALL TEAM. Pictured is Vero's five-man basketball team in their orange and black uniforms. From left to right, they are Sonny Horn, Russ Applegate, Tip Rice, Walter Shelton, and ? Phillips. Local games were played on the Pocahontas Park basketball court. On March 13, 1926, the Vero Beach team participated in the second annual state open championship tournament played in Vero Beach and won against the Jacksonville Greenbacks. (IRCHS.)

POCAHONTAS PARK ZOO, VERO BEACH. Pocahontas Park Zoo acquired its first bear, Alice, in 1925, purchased by Sen. T. J. Campbell for $200. She was small and bad tempered. That same year, a local bobcat was added, captured by James Burrell Tippin. Suzie the bear was donated by Arthur Hill Jr. to be a companion to Alice. Other zoo denizens were alligators, turtles, raccoons, a fox, and an owl. (IRCHS.)

VERO BRIDGE. After years of planning and discussion, in 1919, Vero bridge commissioners set specifications and obtained bids for the construction of the bridge over the Indian River at Vero. It was completed in 1920. After completion, Vero Utilities Company ran power lines over the bridge to light it and to bring power to the Vero Beach Development and the East View Company Development on the barrier islands. (IRCHS.)

VERO BRIDGE GRAND OPENING, 1920. Planning for road construction for access to the bridge site also began in 1919. The road was designed to be a lovely scenic drive from the railroad to the river over the Gifford Road through grove country, then winding north along the Indian River to reach the site for the bridge. (IRCHS.)

Ten

INDIAN RIVER COUNTY

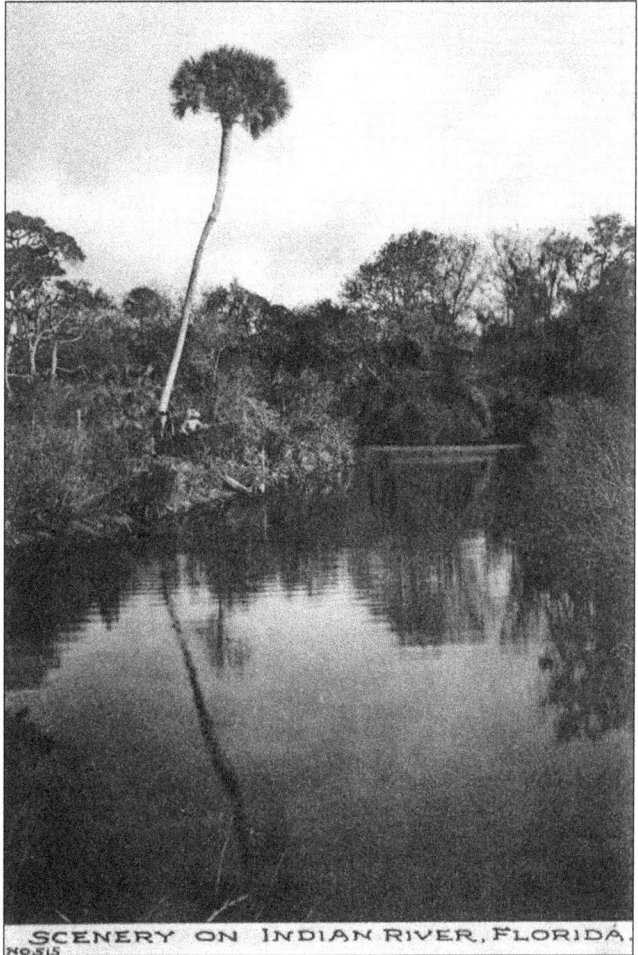

THE INDIAN RIVER. The river for which the county is named runs the length of the eastern part of the county. It is a lagoon and part of the Intracoastal Waterway. It provided the major means of transportation for early inhabitants. Pioneers settled throughout the county, attracted by the fertile land, mild climate, and incredibly diverse ecosystem that was teeming with life. (IRCHS.)

SCENERY ON INDIAN RIVER, FLORIDA.
NO.515

STEAMBOAT ST. LUCIE. This luxury steamboat of the Indian River Steamship Company carried passengers and freight from Titusville to Jupiter on the Indian River in the late 1800s. This company was owned by Jacksonville, Tampa, and Key West Railway, whose trains connected with the steamships at Jupiter to transfer passengers and freight continuing south. Henry Flagler's railroad put both companies out of business in 1895. (IRCHS.)

TOM MORGAN'S PLACE ON SOUTH GIFFORD. Thomas L. Morgan (1846–1933) was born in England and immigrated to Illinois in 1865. He moved to Indian River County prior to 1920. He was a laborer who married and divorced twice with two children each from the two marriages. He is pictured here with his chickens and laundry on the fence on his property in Quay (now Winter Beach). (IRCHS.)

JOSEPH S. AND RUTH S. McCLINTOCK, QUAY.
The McClintocks were readers in the Christian
Science church every Wednesday. Joseph grew
citrus and vegetables. He was a principal in the
Beachland Development Company and secretary
of the commissioners of the Quay Bridge District
in 1923. At the 1920 county fair, Ruth won three
first prizes for her canned vegetables. She was
recording secretary of the Aladdin Club. (IRCHS.)

QUAY SCHOOL, 6500 OLD DIXIE HIGHWAY. In July 1894, Fred and Josephine Chaffey deeded
land for the Quay school to the board of public instruction. This school was built in 1919 with
renovations done in 1927 to enlarge it with more classrooms. As Quay changed its name to
Winter Beach, the school also changed its name to the Winter Beach School. Later it became
the Pleasant Ridge School. It still stands. (IRCHS.)

QUAY BRIDGE, EARLY 1920S. Proposals were accepted by the Quay Bridge District commissioners in March 1923 for the bridge's construction. This bridge remained in operation until it was torn down in the 1950s. No bridge has been built there to replace it. This wooden bridge had a swing span that was operated by a bridge tender. The bridge tender's house can be seen on the right in the background. (IRCHS.)

QUAY RAILROAD STATION, LOOKING SOUTH. This station was built as a produce and freight depot by the Florida East Coast Railway some time between 1894 and 1898 on the east side of the tracks south of Winter Beach Road. It has had many uses: train station, housing for immigrant workers, and fruit stand. It is now a private residence in Roseland where it was relocated in 1976. (IRCHS.)

GEORGE B. HALL'S KLONDIKE GROVE. The Klondike Plantations began approximately 11 miles west of Woodley. The Klondike name has now vanished from the area, as have the names of Woodley and Quay for the town of Winter Beach. Plantations were owned by George B. Hall, Judge Minor S. Jones, E. W. Hall, and John C. Jones. Judge Jones was the first, with land purchased in the late 1890s. (SIE.)

HALL IN HIS FRONT YARD, KLONDIKE PLANTATIONS. Sometime before April 1900, George B. Hall obtained a Klondike plantation, which he planted with orange groves. He also planted vegetables. He had a large potato crop and cucumbers. By the first of November 1900, he had moved onto his Klondike property from his home in Sebastian. That same month, he shipped his first crop of oranges. (SIE.)

GEORGE HALL AND MANGO TREE, KLONDIKE. In addition to Judge Jones and George Hall, there were a few other Klondikers. In March 1901, tax collector E. W. Hall sold his orange groves at Sharpes in order to concentrate on his Klondike groves. Postmaster John C. Jones, son of Judge Jones, had a 20-acre orange grove and farm. Seminole Indians Billy Smith, Polly Parker, and her granddaughter were frequent visitors. (SIE.)

JAMES J. ROBERTS HOME, VERO, C. 1916. The original Roberts home was a 14-foot-by-20-foot shack along the Dixie Highway, the first for many miles around in 1901. James started by planting vegetables, which in turn paid for his orange and grapefruit groves that he began planting in 1903. His home was relocated and renovated by C. A. Prang in 1916 facing Dixie Highway a mile south of Vero. (IRCHS.)

FRED T. LOCKWOOD PLANTING YOUNG TREES, JANUARY 2, 1917. Fred Lockwood and his wife, Florence, came to Florida in 1914 from Michigan. He was a pioneer citrus grower in the area. Their daughter Charlotte was a renowned local historian and author of three books. Her book *Florida's Historic Indian River County* incorporated much of her father's collection of photographs and documents pertaining to the early history of the county. (IRCHS.)

PACKINGHOUSE. By 1919, local citrus packinghouses had to expand to keep up with the industry growth. Herman Davis's new plant in Oslo could pack two railroad cars a day. Vero Packing House enlarged to handle five cars a day. Deerfield Company in Wabasso packed five cars daily, and Storch Brothers at Sebastian handled four to five daily. The total was expected to double in two years. (IRCHS.)

CITRUS CRATES, *SEALD SWEET*, VERO. The Florida Citrus Exchange was created in 1909 based on the California Exchange model. In 1915, George Scott of the Boston office suggested using a representative name for the Florida Citrus Exchange fruit. Seald Sweet was the name tested by Thomas Advertising that proved most effective. This was adopted by the exchange board, and its first trademark, Sealdsweet, was obtained in October 1915. (IRCHS.)

FRUIT GROWERS ASSOCIATION, PHOTOGRAPHED BY ROY WAKER. The citrus shipping figures for the season were published February 12, 1921, in the *Vero Press*. The Vero Fruit Growers Association shipped 30 train cars of fruit, with 15 or 20 cars shipped from other sources in Vero. American Fruit Growers plant at Wabasso shipped 153 cars, and Oslo Packing Company plant shipped 44 cars. Fellsmere and Quay figures were not available. (IRCHS.)

HALLSTROM HOUSE, OSLO. The Hallstrom's first house was a small two-room wooden-frame building constructed in 1910, which still stands on the east side of Old Dixie Highway. In 1915–1918, Axel Hallstrom built a two-story brick house across the street with five bedrooms. It still exists, surrounded by 5 acres, and is now maintained by Indian River County Historical Society. It is on the National Register of Historic Places. (IRCHS-HH.)

RUTH HALLSTROM, GRADUATION, FORT PIERCE HIGH SCHOOL, 1921. Ruth Hallstrom's graduation dress was made by her aunt Johanna Hallstrom. After graduation, Ruth taught, and then spent a year in finishing school in Sweden. In 1910, Johanna came to live with Ruth and her father, Axel, when his wife, Emily, died. Ruth was four at the time. Axel was a pineapple and citrus grower. (IRCHS-HH.)

HALLSTROM PINEAPPLES. Axel Hallstrom first created a pineapple plantation in Viking, which he sold in 1910. That same year, he purchased 40 acres from the Kroegels at 50¢ an acre and had it cleared and planted in pineapples by late fall. In December 1920, one of Axel Hallstorm's pineapples displayed in the window of Jun's Cash and Carry Grocery Store attracted attention because of its unusual size—5 pounds. (IRCHS-HH.)

EDGAR J. WOOD'S FISH HOUSE AT THE END OF OSLO ROAD. Fishing was only one of Wood's interests. In 1914, Wood opened a general store. He was on the board of trade and the board of realtors, was a bank officer, a car salesman, and was active in community affairs such as a new county dock and preservation of fossil specimens. He held the honorary title of colonel. (IRCHS.)

DIXIE HIGHWAY ALONG THE INDIAN RIVER. The Dixie Highway system was constructed between 1915 and 1927 as a series of interconnected paved roads linking southeast United States to the Midwest. Much of the Old Dixie Highway still remains in Indian River County, partly as U.S. Highway 1 or as State Road 5 or 5A. (IRCHS.)

TIN CAN TOURISTS. Pictured here are some of the "Tin Can Tourists," so-called because of the easy availability and cheap price of World War 1 surplus tents and vehicles. Coupled with the spread of the highway system across America, a new type of tourist was created. These adventuresome souls camped out, ate at roadside stands, and explored unknown byways. (IRCHS.)

BIBLIOGRAPHY

Colberson, James E. *Images, Through the Doors of Time*. Melbourne, FL: Sea Bird Publishing, c. 1995.

Fellsmere Farmer. Fellsmere, FL: Fellsmere Farms Company, 1912–1913.

The Florida Star. Titusville, FL: S. W. Harmon, 1880–1917(?).

Gross, George William. *Tales of Waldo E. Sexton, 1885–1967*. Vero Beach, FL: Sexton, Inc., 2001.

The Indian River Farmer. Chicago, IL: Indian River Farms Company, 1913–1915.

Newman, Anna Pearl Leonard. *Stories of Early Life Along Beautiful Indian River*. Stuart, FL: *Stuart Daily News*, 1953.

Patterson, Gordon. "Ditches and Dreams, Nelson Fell and the Rise of Fellsmere." *Florida Historical Quarterly*, (summer 1997): 1–20.

Robinson, Tim. *A Tropical Frontier, Pioneers and Settlers of Southeast Florida, 1800–1890*. Port Salerno, FL: Port Sun Publishing, 2005.

The Saint Lucie County Tribune (Saint Lucie Tribune). Fort Pierce, FL: Wilson and Reed, 1920.

Sebastian River Area Historical Society, Inc. *Tales of Sebastian*. Sebastian, FL: Sebastian River Area Historical Society, Inc. 1990.

Vero Beach, Florida, City Directory. Vol. 1, 1927–1928. Asheville, NC: Florida-Piedmont Directory Company, Publishers, 1927.

Vero Press [Press Journal]. Vero Beach, FL: Vero Press, 1919–1925.

Vertical Files. Indian River County History, Archive Center, Indian River County Main Library. Vero Beach, FL.

Wagner, Kip, and L. B. Taylor Jr. *Pieces of Eight: Recovering the Riches of a Lost Spanish Treasure Fleet*. Port Salerno, FL: Florida Classics Library, 1998.

INDEX

1715 Spanish Plate Fleet, 15
Andrews, Judge James E., 85
Ashley Gang, 25
Baptist Church, 106
Barber, Merrill, 93
Baker, James Hudson, 90, 110
Barker's Bluff, 29, 30
Barker family, 11
Bethel Creek House of Refuge, 20
Cail family, 69, 70
Carter, Robert D., 44, 86
Commerce Avenue, 101
Dawson family, 10
Dinky Train, 53
Dixie Highway, 69, 101, 125
Ercildoune, 22, 23
Farmer's Bank, 98, 101
Fell family, 42
Fellsmere Estates Corporation, 61
Fleming Grant, 21, 27
Forster, Frank, 11, 12, 13
Gem Island, 10
Gifford family, 97
Graves Brothers, 28, 84
Hallstrom family, 123, 124
Hardee family, 36
Jackson, William Henry, 26, 30
Johns Island, 15
Jun's Grocery, 99, 103, 124
Kitching family, 33, 36
Klondike Plantations, 119, 120
Kroegel, Paul, 9, 30, 31, 34
Lawson family, 32, 34
MacWilliam, Alec, 16
Maher 99, 103
Marian Fell Library, 63
Marsh Landing Restaurant, 61

Michael family, 12, 13, 14
Orchid Island, 11–14
Park family, 33
Pelican Island, 9
Pocahontas Park, 99, 113
Riomar, 16
San Sebastian, 23
Sears family, 69, 70
Seminole Building, 99, 102
Sexton, Waldo, 17, 89
Sleepy Eye Lodge, 88- 90, 102
Smith family, 70, 71, 72, 76
Trimble, Frederick H., 61
Vandiveer family, 73–76, 78, 79
Vero Press, 100
Vickers family, 32, 33, 59
Waker family, 94, 95
Walker, Eli C., 108, 110
Woman's Club, 107
Wigfield family, 12, 13
Young family, 92
Zeuch, Herman, 16, 86

Visit us at
arcadiapublishing.com

www.ingramcontent.com/pod-product-compliance
Lightning Source LLC
Chambersburg PA
CBHW050637110426
42813CB00007B/1834